Concise Text Book of Research Methods for Theological Education

Concise Text Book of Research Methods for Theological Education

An Introduction

Shyam K. Basumatary

Christian World Imprints

First Published in 2025 by

Christian World Imprints
Christian Publishing & Books from India
A-71 Group, Wazirpur Industrial Area
Delhi-110052
cwidelhi2017@gmail.com
www.ChristianWorldImprints.com
Phone: +91 11 41526079

ISBN: 978-93-6065-903-5 (HB)
ISBN: 978-93-6065-189-3 (PB)

Printed in India.

Contents

Preface

During my Master of Theology study at the United Theological College, Bengaluru, in 1998-2000, one of my student friends came to me asked me "Shyam, what is methodology?" I explained him about methodology what I knew then. As I reflect back it was far from clear what I explained about method and methodology. As students we used to experience butterfly in our stomach when we had Inter-Disciplinary paper in front of faculty members and students from all departments. Students from Christian Ministry were the ones who used to receive sharp criticisms from all corners.

For the last one decade I have been teaching the subject "Research Methods" at the Master of Theology level at Eastern Theological College under the Senate of Serampore College (University). The more I teach the more I came to learn that this area of study is difficult for theological students. Coming from theological background without any specialized technical knowledge on the subject makes me humbler in attempting to write on the subject area. Only consolation that I have is I had little experience in empirical study during the study of Master of Theology programme at rudimentary level in the form of questionnaire and content analysis.

Research Method is a technical, theoretical, conceptual and empirical subject. Without empirical experience, it is difficult to comprehend the various social research methods. In theological education different disciplines have their own methodologies, but when it comes to empirical study all disciplines have to use social science research methods, primarily either quantitative or qualitative or both.

There is apparent confusion among the theological fraternity in the difference between method and methodology. Sometime even writing style or method, like footnote and bibliography are considered methodology, which is not the case. Writing method or style and method and methodology are entirely different from each other, although there is close connection between them. In theological education while other disciplines depend on their respective methodologies, research on Christian ministry basically depends on social science research methods. In a sense research on Christian ministry department heavily relies on empirical study.

This book attempts to provide a general theoretical understanding of social research methods in theological education, particularly in Christian ministry. The book consists of 15 chapters based on the syllabus "Research Methods" for the degree of Master of Theology under the Senate of Serampore College (University). It is a seminal work, attempting to offer salient features of social science research methods for the aspiring Bachelor of Divinity students, Master of Theology students and Research Scholars. There is ample scope to develop and enlarge the work. I hope the book will function as a wedge to open up new vistas and encourage aspiring research scholars to take further lead in theological education.

Shyam K. Basumatary

Introduction

In theological research, particularly in the department of Christian ministry research, method is an integral part of research process. There are various types of research methods. Although, in theological research we may not use all those methods, however having a fare knowledge of various research methods is helpful for a researcher. In theological research, each discipline has its own method and methodology, however research of Christian ministry heavily relies on social science research methods. There are mainly two aspects in the method of Christian ministry, namely – theoretical and empirical. Theoretical aspect of the method in Christian ministry is based on various models, theories and therapies of the respective disciplines. It is also based on extensive literature review or survey. Out of theoretical aspect theoretical or conceptual framework is developed.

Empirical aspect is based on empirical study. Empirical study is based on *observation* and *experience.* Empirical study is scientific study, based on popularly known as "social science" methods. Empiricism is a way of knowing and understanding the world that relies directly or indirectly on what we experience through our senses – sight, hearing, taste, smell and touch. In other words, in empiricism information or data can be acceptable insofar it can be observed or sensed in someway specifiable conditions. It does not depend on authority, revelation, intuition or other nonnumerical ways of knowing the world or any phenomenon, which may be acceptable in theology and philosophy. Scientists do not accept any conclusion or generalization based on authority, tradition or common sense. In empirical study evidence is paramount. Any scientific study will ask whether or not it is empirically resolvable. If it is not, then it is beyond the realm of science (Singleton and Strait. *Approaches to Social Research,* Third Edition. New York; Oxford: Oxford University Press, 1999).

Till the middle of the nineteenth century the study of society and social phenomena was done under philosophy and history. It was done mostly based on speculation, logic, theological thinking and rational analysis. August Comte, a French philosopher, described these methods were inadequate and insufficient in the study of social life. So, in 1848, he propounded a method called, *positive method* in the study of social research. He argued that social phenomena cannot be studied through logic or theological principle or metaphysical theories but should be done in the society itself in and through the structure of the social relations. This is where the study of society in the form of *sociology* came into existence. For example, the study of poverty in sociology would examine the forces that caused poverty. This new method is called *positivism.* This method has rejected the speculative and philosophical theories in the study of society. Rather the study on society focussed on empirical data and became *positivist methodology* similar to natural science. By 1930s, the positivist method became popular in United States of America and other countries as well.

However, this method was criticized heavily from within and outside of the field. Frankfurt and Marxism schools sharply criticized the method. Interconnectionism, phenomenology and ethnomethodology also criticised, despite giving new name of *logical positivism.* Still it became popular in 1950s and 1960s in academics, particularly in the west. Today new trend called post-empiricist claims that scientific empiricist is not the only source of knowledge, truth and validity. As a result, *post-positivist* method was developed that holds the view that positivist is not only method to study reality of society but there are diverse methods and techniques by which social research can be done. Now therefore, there are two approaches to study society – scientific empirical method and naturalist phenomenological method. The scientific empirical methods are employed in an attempt to establish general law or principle, which is also called *nomothetic,* which assumes that social reality is objective with a focus on quantitative analysis. This approach, with focus on individual rather than general law-making is termed as *ideographic* approach (Burns, Robert B. *Introduction to Research Methods,* 4th edition. London; Thousand Oaks; New Delhi: SAGE Publications, 2000).

The study of psychology as an autonomous discipline also started in the middle of the nineteenth century. In the study of psychology in relation to education, the role of empiricism came into play in various developmental theories, to the extent that its role has become inevitable in the discipline of Christian ministry. Jean Piaget is considered the first empiricist in education. Based on empirical study he developed "cognitive development theory" (Piaget, Jean. *Six Psychological Studies.* New York: Vintage Books, 1967). There on based on his empiricism various developmental theories were developed. Among them, Lawrence Kohlberg's "Moral Development" (Kohlberg, Lawrence, *The Psychology of Moral Development and the Idea of Justice.* San Francisco, Toronto: Harper & Raw, 1984) and James Fowler's "Faith Development" (Fowler, James W. *Stages of Faith: The*

Psychology of Human Development and the Quest for Meaning. San Francisco: Harper & Row, 1981) theories are notable. Both of them developed their developmental theories based on Piaget's theory. On the other hand, Erik H. Erikson developed his "psychosocial or emotional" (Erikson, Erik H. *Identity and Life Cycle.* New York: International University Press, 1959) development theory based on Freud's "psychoanalysis" theory. Despite theological education being metaphysical and transcendental, we can see over reliance on empiricism or social science method in the study of Christian ministry.

This book attempts to offer a general introduction of various research methods of social science at the theoretical and conceptual level. Except in few cases, I have omitted mathematical aspect due to lack of my expertise. However, the book attempts to deal with basic components of social science research methods based on the syllabus "Research Methods" for the degree of Master of Theology in the department of Christian Ministry under the Senate of Serampore College (University).

Chapter 1

Approach to Social Science Research

Introduction

The word "science" is derived from Latin *Scientia* which means "knowledge." The main aim of science is to produce knowledge to understand and explain the reality of the world around us. But there is difference between scientific knowledge and common knowledge in the understanding of the world. There is chasm between scientific understanding and common sense. As a result, there exists difference between science and common sense. Common sense depends upon the community life embedded in different cultural elements and practices, by which human beings try to make sense out of things they come across in their day to day life. The common sense may be capitulated with prejudices and different belief systems, which often can be sometime contradictory and inconsistent. However, scientific knowledge is based on verifiable evidence or systematic body of proof. For example, a prejudiced statement may say tribal people are less intelligent than general caste people, or men are more intelligent than women. But contrary to this statement the scientific study may find that tribal and general and men and women are equally intelligent. Science does not take anything for granted, as Albert Einstein rightly said "Not everything that can be counted counts, and not everything that counts can be counted." According to Kerlinger cited by Ahuja, science and common sense differ from each other as follows:

1. Difference between Science and Common Sense

1.1. Use of Conceptual Schemes

Both science and common sense use conceptual scheme. However, the difference is that a common person may take things loosely, but scientist will build his/her conceptual scheme systematically with theoretical structure and consistency.

1.2. Empirical Test

The scientist tests his/her hypothesis and theories systematically through empirical testing, whereas a common person may select evidence that suits his/her hypothesis. For day to day life, a common person depends on common sense prevalent in the community. Scientific inquiry is not *a priori* for common people.

1.3. Notion of Control

The notion of control means a scientist will choose those variables that can be hypothesized and provide 'causes' but rules out those that are 'possible causes' of effects of a phenomenon under study. A layperson seldom controls any variables or sources that influence the phenomenon under study. Contrary, the scientist will not be influenced by those extraneous factors but control them.

1.4. Relation of Phenomena

In terms of relation of phenomena there is sharp difference between science and common sense as both talk of relation. However, a scientist will consciously and systematically pursue the relation, while a layperson does not do that way. A layperson's relation can be loose, unsystematic and uncontrolled.

1.5. Explanation of Observed Phenomena

A scientist will rule out any philosophical and metaphysical (and theological) elements in the explanation of a phenomenon, that which cannot be tested. For example, an assumption that certain people groups are poor because of their laziness. But social scientist will not come to that sort of conclusion without the proper and in-depth study of the socio-economic and political situations of the people groups. The social scientist will study causes and effect of poverty. Science, particularly natural science will describe any reality as it is. It is more concerned with the question of what "it is" than why "it is."

2. Characteristic of Scientific Research

Horton and Hunt (1984) provide the following characteristics of scientific research:

a. *Verifiable evidence*: This is factual observation which other than the researcher also can observe and check. By observing and checking others also can verify the findings. A researcher may claim to arrive at certain truth or conclusion but science will look for validity and reliability. Unless and until there is verifiable evidence in any research the scientist will not draw conclusion.

b. *Accuracy*: The scientific research describes any phenomenon exactly it really exists. Truth and correctness of statement derived out of the research process are exactly described without jumping to unwarranted conclusion. Before drawing any conclusion, a scientist will verify the findings.

c. *Precision*: Precision is giving exact number rather than vague information. For example, in the empirical study of any research for youth, instead of saying "I have distributed my questionnaire to many youths," the researcher would say "I have distributed the questionnaire to 100 youth." In scientific research "many," "majority," or "much" etc. do not suffice. Data should be accurate and precise.

d. *Systematization*: It is collecting all the relevant data systematically and organizing data so that conclusion drawn will be reliable with sound judgement. The scientific research should not and cannot be done haphazardly. The researcher has to collect data systematically and organize properly. The researcher has to ensure whether or not data collected are relevant and useful.

e. *Objectivity*: In any social science research, the researcher has to pay paramount importance to objectivity. It means being free from biases and prejudices. It is observing a particular research undertaken which is free from observer's value, beliefs and preferences. It is free from the opinion of the researcher. The researcher presents his/her facts and findings objectively. Objectivity means that empirical evidence of any scientific study exists outside of scientists themselves. Objectivity is free from emotion, conjecture or personal biases. However, absolute objectivity is a myth. Therefore, social psychologists say that we do not see the world "as is." Rather we learn how to see. So, scientists assign a limited and far more useful meaning attached to the term "objective." To scientists it is observation of a group of scientists. It means two or more scientists are observing the same condition to agree that they are observing the same thing or event. The technical term used for this is called "intersubjective testability." Ultimately, objectivity is a product of community of thinkers (Nagel, 1967).

f. *Recording*: Recording is one aspect that a scientist can never ignore or overlook. In the process of research, recording the details of the findings is inevitable. A scientist will record by jotting down in complete details the finding at his/her disposal. A scientist does not rely on memory because our memory is fallible. Researcher will not depend on recalled facts but will analyse the problem based on recorded facts. For research, we cannot rely on memory. To remember everything is neither possible nor desirable.

g. *Controlling conditions*: Control means eliminating bias and errors as far as possible that may distort result of scientific inquiry. When we do research we need to be mindful of myriad conditions that we come across. Research will depend on how we control these conditions. In any given research, there will be many variables that we need to control. A natural scientist is able to control many variables as he/she wishes in experiment, say – heat, light, air pressure, time interval etc. but social scientist cannot control all variables as he/she wishes. For example, if the social scientist wants to study behaviour of students in classroom, the students' behaviour will depend on various factors, such as – teacher's efficiency and communication skill, availability of books, fan, proper light, physical environment etc. However, to be completely free from the influence of bias is impossible. Even selection of problem for study and preference for certain strategy and methods carry subjectivity. But a scientist will try to control and minimize as much as possible in the process of scientific inquiry. The principle of control lies behind virtually in the procedure and technique in the process of scientific inquiry.

h. *Training investigators*: In certain research project help of others is unavoidable. We will be bound to take help from investigators whom at times training will be required. So, training investigators means imparting necessary knowledge to investigators about the research undertaken and how to interpret data accurately. The scientist will first try to know the level of education, training, sophistication etc. of the investigator(s) and ask question like "Does he/she really understand the facts he/she reports? If the investigators are not competent enough the research will not reach to desired goal.

Citing Black and Champion (1960), Henry Johnson outlines the following characteristics of social science research:

a. It is empirical, that is based on observation and reasoning and not on speculation.
b. It is theoretical, that it summarizes data with precision giving logical relationship between propositions which explain causal relationship.
c. It is cumulative, that is generalization/theories are corrected, rejected and new developed theories are built upon one another.
d. It is non-ethical, that is scientists do not say whether particular things/events/phenomena/institutions/

systems/structures are good or bad. They just explain. It is value free.

Robert E. Burns (2000), further brings out four characteristics of scientific research – control, operational definition, replication and hypothesis testing. *Control* eliminates simultaneous influences of many variables and isolate the cause and effect in order to provide unambiguous answers. *Operational definition* means it must be defined in terms of steps to measure them. *Replication* means repeated study to obtain reliable data. *Hypothesis testing* means, the researcher systematically creates a hypothesis and subjects it to empirical test.

3. Aims of Social Science Research

The aims of social research depend on the type of research, that is – exploratory, explanatory, descriptive research etc. The following aims can be broadly considered:

a. To understand the functioning of society.
b. To study the individual behaviour and social action.
c. To evaluate social problems, their effects on society, and to find out possible solutions.
d. To explore social reality and explain social life.
e. To develop theories.

Becker and (1989) and Sarantakos (1998) offer the following goals:

a. *General goal*: Understanding for its own sake.
b. *Theoretical goal*: Verification, falsification, modification or discovery of theory.
c. *Pragmatic goals*: Solution of social problems.
d. *Political goal*: Development of social policy, evaluation of programmes, planning of reconstruction, empowerment and liberation.

Sometime goals coincide with motives. The motives can be *intrinsic* and sometime it can be *extrinsic.* Mahr outlined the following motives.

e. Educational motive to educate and inform public.
f. Personal motive to promote the academic status of the researcher. This kind of research can be geared toward academic pursuit of an individual to earn degree in enhancing own carrier.
g. Institutional motive to enhance the research quantum of the institution for which the researcher works. A church, institution, convention or organization may entrust someone to study to develop, improve and evaluate their activities.
h. Political motive to support for political plan and programmes. This kind of goal can be found in the study of political goal of a particular political party.
i. Tactical motive to make decision or to act on certain issues in the process of investigation in a given research.

Summary

There are two kinds of scientific research, namely – natural science research and social science research. There is difference between scientific knowledge and common sense. Scientific research has verifiable evidence, accuracy, precision, and objectivity. Social science is empirically based on observation and reasoning and not on speculation. It is cumulative and non-ethical. The aim is to understand an individual, community and society and evaluate social issues/ problems in order to find solution and develop theories.

References

Ahuja, Ram. *Research Method.* New Delhi: Rawat Publications, 2011.

Black, James and Dem Champion. *Methods and Issues in Social Research.* New York: John Wiley and Sons, 1976.

Burns, Robert E. *Introduction to Research Methods,* 4th edition. London, Thousand Oaks, New Delhi, 2000.

Kerlinger, Fred N. *Foundations of Social Behaviour.* New York: Holt, Rinehart and Winston Inc., 1964.

Sarantakos, S. *Social Research,* 2nd edition. London: Macmillan Press, 1998.

Singleton, Jr. Royce A. and Bruce C. Straight. *Approaches to Social Research,* Third Edition. New York; Oxford: Oxford University Press, 1999.

Patton, Michael Quinn. *Qualitative Research & Evaluation Methods,* Third Edition. Thousand Oaks; London; New Delhi: SAGE Publications, 2002.

Chapter 2

Conventional/Traditional Research and Participatory Action Research Logic and Structure

Introduction

There are two broad categories of research methods – Conventional or Traditional Research Method and Participatory Action Research method. Based on these two categories of research methods we can find different types of research methods. In this chapter our discussion will be on Conventional/Traditional Research method and Participatory Action Research method and their Logic and Structure. Before, we go into detail of our discussion; let us first see the meaning and definition of research and method.

1. Definition of Research

The term "Research" is derived from the French word *recherche.* Hunter P Mabry defines Research as "a careful investigation of a phenomenon with an objective of advancing and enhancing knowledge." It is a systematic investigation to find solutions to a problem. In simple way we can say that research is the search for an answer to a problem. It is re-searching solution/answer to a problem.

According Ram Ahuja "Research is a careful and exhaustive investigation of a phenomenon with an objective of advancing knowledge." For Theodorson and Theodorson "it is systematic and objective attempt to study a problem for the purpose of deriving general principles." Robert B. Burns describes it as a systematic investigation to find solution to a problem.

According to American sociologist Earl Robert Babbie, "Research is a systematic inquiry to describe, explain, predict and control observed phenomenon." It is the creation of new knowledge and/or the use of existing knowledge in a new and different way so as to generate new concepts, methodologies and understanding. Research is a systematic investigation into and study of materials and sources in order to establish facts and reach new conclusion. It is a careful consideration of study regarding a particular concern or problem using scientific method. It is a careful consideration of study regarding a particular concern or problem using scientific method.

Again, research can be divided mainly into two types of research, social science research and natural science research. Theological education, particularly in Christian ministry research is done based on social science research. Natural scientist and social scientist differ from each other as follows: A natural scientist (1) does not participate in the phenomenon he/she studies (2) does not conduct interview (3) has a liberty for conducting experiment (4) use instrument and chemicals in experiment (5) can control many variables in his/her experiment. Whereas social scientist (1) participate in the study of phenomenon (2) conduct interviews or questionnaire to collect data (3) has no laboratory for testing

(4) does not use any instrument (5) cannot control many variables.

2. Method

Method is a particular procedure for approaching and completing something, especially as systematic or established one. It is a process for attaining an object. It is a systematic procedure, technique, or mode of inquiry employed by or proper to particular discipline or art.

3. Difference between Method and Methodology

There is difference between method and methodology. Method is a tool or technique of process to collect data for research undertaken. It is a procedure used to obtain knowledge based on empirical observation and logical reasoning to draw conclusion. Methodology is on the other hand study of method in particular research. It is a logic of scientific investigation. It means description, explanation, justification of methods used in the research, not the methods themselves. It is a theory of analysis of the whole research project. Methods are like survey method, experimental method, case-study method, statistical method and so on. Methodology is concerned with technique used to collect data. It requires potentialities and limitations with one or the other. Methodology is a plan and procedure for carrying out research. It deals with research techniques and strategies in obtaining valid information. It is an approach to understand a phenomenon and procedure of empirical investigation. Methodology is not concerned with building knowledge but concerned with how knowledge is built, how facts are collected, classified and analysed. Methodology deals with the question of *how,* whereas method deals with the question of *what* the research procedure is. In simple term the difference between method and methodology can be defined by "dialogue" and "dialogical" in educational setting, where dialogue refers to method and dialogical to methodology.

4. What is Logic?

Logic simply means reasoning. It generally refers to any system of rules for thoughts and expression, thus leading to some action. It deals with the principles, methods and criteria of correct reasoning or distinguishing correct from incorrect arguments/statement/conclusion etc. It deals with the relationship between evidence and conclusion. It is concerned with the coherency between evidence and conclusion. It is concerned with the adequacy of the evidence to affirm conclusion. While, in scientific field, certain ways of reasoning may be acceptable, others may not be acceptable. The aim of logic is to state the principles upon which this distinction is made. In order to understand and accept the scientific observations, we have to understand these principles of reasoning. Logic tells us whether evidence justifies the conclusion. The goal of logic is to evaluate reasoning.

There are generally three major types of reasoning – deductive, inductive and abductive.

4.1. Deductive Reasoning: Conclusion Guaranteed

Deductive reasoning means when a person presents his/her claim as true conclusion if all the premises are true. Deductive reasoning starts with assertion of general rule and proceeds to specific conclusion. Deductive reasoning moves from general rule to specific conclusion. In the deductive reasoning if the original premises/assumption/assertion is true then conclusion also must be true. We see deductive reasoning in mathematics. For example, two plus two is equal to four.

4.2. Inductive Reasoning: Conclusion Merely likely/ Possibility

Inductive reasoning means if a person claims conclusion is true but not necessarily even if all the premises are true. Simply put in Inductive reasoning your claim of conclusion can be true even if all premises are not necessarily true. Inductive reasoning starts from specific to general. It starts with observation that is specific and limited in scope proceeds to a generalized conclusion that is likely but not certain. Most of the social research is done through inductive reasoning. For example, if the research is done among a specific sub-tribe within a larger tribe, the finding or conclusion need not be necessarily true or applicable for the entire tribe.

4.3. Abductive Reasoning

In abductive reasoning you take the best shot. It starts with an incomplete set of observations and proceeds to likeliest possible explanation and conclusion. This kind of reasoning is used in our daily activities and in our decision-making process. Without going into detail, we arrive at certain decision with the best possible information at hand, which is often incomplete. In medical service abductive reasoning is used. For example, a patient may not be able to explain or give information of all the symptoms he/she is having, but the physician will affirm/conclude the sickness based on whatever available information he/she gets. It is also used by jurors. A juror may not get all the evidences needed for verdict, but comes to best possible conclusion whatever evidences available at hand. For such case they use circumstantial evidence.

5. Logical Analysis: Its Elements

Now the question before us is how do we analyse any particular research logically? Citing Singleton and Straits,

Ram Ahuja outlines three fundamental logical analyses: *terms, propositions* and *arguments.*

5.1. Term

A term is a word with a specific meaning. Some terms are antecedent, syllogism, valid argument, induction etc. In science, terms are analogous to concept. Antecedent means a thing that existed before or logically proceeds to the next. Syllogism means a form of reasoning by which conclusion is drawn from two or more assumed propositions or premises. A common or middle term is present in two premises but not in conclusion. For example, *all dogs are animals: all animals have four legs: therefore, all dogs have four legs.*

5.2. Proposition

A proposition is the meaning of a sentence. The meaning of the sentence is different from sentence itself. Proposition could be either true or false. The proposition can be conditional or categorical. Conditional is based on 'if' and 'when,' but the categorical does not provide any room for condition. Sometime we say 'categorical statement' or 'categorical proposition.' For example, all heavy things fall on earth is a categorical proposition, while in case of sale of products conditional proposition will say "if the advertisement is good it will add on the sale."

5.3. Argument

Argument is a group of two or more propositions, followed by one by the other(s). For example, "John failed in exam, because he did not study hard." The cause of failure is explained on the argument that John did not study hard. The proposition which is affirmed is called 'conclusion,' while the one that supplies evidence is known as 'premise.' Argument given by logician/researcher is called 'syllogism.'

6. Structure

The *structure* of any inquiry/research means what the different parts of a research are, how they connect with each other, what will be done in the research and in what sequence. In simple way, we can say structure means what we are looking for, how are we going to get/achieve it, what data are needed, and how they will be collected. It is pre-specifying everything in advance. In structure the research questions, the design, and method(s) of data collection all worked out in advance. A set of steps is laid and the researcher proceeds according to those steps. Structure is the outline, the scheme, the paradigm of the operation of the variables. It involves image of various parts, components or elements, original, organized into unity. The general concept of structure can be observed in human activities, for instance, in family, an army, and institution.

7. Conventional or Traditional Method

Conventional method also can be called Traditional Method. This particular method was used particularly by anthropologists during the modern era. It is used in anthropology, travelogue, ethnography etc. In this method of research, the members and communities of the party involved are treated as passive objects, where the area of participation of people is confined to the extent of authorizing projects, being objects and receiving the results. Here the people on whom the research is done are considered as mere objects. Traditional or Conventional method is also called Experimental method.

This Traditional Method has been dominant in academic community. It is oriented toward making our knowledge within the subject area more completed, either by seeking to fill the gaps or resolve the problems within the existing corpus of knowledge, or by re-examining some parts of accepted knowledge, where the researcher believes questionable or perhaps in need of revision. The purpose of inquiry in this model is 'pursuit of truth.' The truth is conceptualized, abstractly or theoretically, as being unified body of knowledge.

The researchers who follow this method consider themselves as academic scholars whose primary task is to generate and investigate new knowledge to make complete and more unified one. Here the researcher tries to be detached observer. It is done through quantitative method. The researcher tries to stand outside of the phenomenon being studied. Ideally the researcher personally remains uninvolved and attempts to perceive 'facts' objectively. This method is found to be helpful in filling many gaps in human knowledge. In its refined form, this research is oriented toward the construction of an abstract theoretical schema which provide conceptual framework for understanding one's own subject area.

7.1. Conventional/Traditional Research as Pure Research

The Traditional Research is considered as Pure Research. This research is called basic research. It is concerned with development, examination, verification and refinement of research methods, procedures and tools that form the body of research methodology. It is the formal and systematic process. It seeks to increase the volume of knowledge. This research is referred to as 'domain driven' which is intended for theoretical development.

7.2. Conventional/Traditional Research as Experimental or Quantitative Research

The Conventional or Traditional research adopts experiment in natural science as the model of scientific research. The conventional or traditional research, thus, can be termed as experimental or quantitative research. The logic of this research is for collecting data using standardized approaches. In this research, researchers use quantitative method, which is an umbrella term covering different types of research. In its simplest form it is concerned with frequently things happened and the presentation of these frequencies as summarized in tables, charts, graphs, figures etc. In traditional scientific research, the scientist/researcher claims that he/she is disinterested and unbiased observer who can produce objective truth about reality. Therefore, social science, which follows this tradition, aims to make social research as natural science, such as physics and chemistry. This kind of research is also called positivist research.

7.3. Conventional/Traditional Research as Subjectivity

To be subjective means to be biased, prejudiced, unreliable and irrational. Subjectivity implies opinion rather than facts, intuition rather than logic, impression rather than confirmation. The task of conventional research is to control subjectivity and maintain objectivity as best as possible way. Trying to maintain objectivity or to reach to objectivity to the maximum possible through quantitative method is the task of conventional research. Quantitative methods are, of course, no more synonymous with objectivity than qualitative methods are synonymous with subjectivity. In other words, qualitative research is synonymous with subjectivity, while quantitative method is no more synonymous with objectivity. Although, conventional research through quantitative method attempts to be objective as best as possible, elements of subjectivity cannot be ruled out entirely.

7.4. Strengths and Weaknesses of Traditional Research

a. Strengths

i. It is oriented toward increasing or strengthening knowledge in a specific area and gives attention to bring positive change among the people being studied.

ii. Traditional model of research is dominant within academic community. It is goal oriented and purposive.

iii. Traditional paradigm takes into consideration to the self-perceived needs of the people being studied.

iv. By virtue of formal training in the academic community, the researcher is able to present the research technically in a traditional way.

v. This research is expressed in technical, professional academic language in the form of reports, theses and dissertations.

b. Weaknesses

i. It tends to be abstract in form and style and written in esoteric language which is inaccessible to others.

ii. This kind of research is concentrated on narrowly defined areas, which may be of interest to some persons and not to the wider audience.

iii. It is mainly confined within academic need for securing degrees.

iv. It treats people as objects.

v. The oppressed are identified, measured, dissected and analyzed from outside and the result is not discussed with the people being studied.

vi. Complete/absolute objectivity is a myth. Total non-involvement, detached observation, complete value free research is impossible. No matter, how might we may claim to be objective, we cannot rule out the elements of subjectivity entirely, because *observer* is part of the *observed* and *signifier* is part of the *signified.*

vii. Feminist movements and women's studies say it is seriously flawed because it is male biased or androcentric in most of the theoretical framework.

viii. In India, the Dalits, Tribals, Adivasis and Social movements find problematic, because national political parties, the educational structure, the state bureaucracy, the arms forces and commerce are still dominated by high caste.

8. Participatory Action Research

Participatory Action Research has been understood by different names, such as – Action Research, Practitioner Research, Participative Enquiry, Participatory Learning, Participatory Action and Research. As the name suggests Participatory Action allows people in the community or organization under study to participate actively along with the researcher throughout research process from the beginning till the end. In this research, people are not passive but active participators in the research process. It is research *with* people, not research *on* people. In this research, the researcher takes the people along with him/her. The aim is to enable participants share their understanding of the problem and find solution to it. In a sense it is democratic in its approach. In this research, people get opportunity to learn through participation rather than having just idea of facts and truths about the problem. Therefore, this research has advantage in giving solution to the problem as it involves those community members who understand the problem and issue better. Because of this, people will own the research and will feel that it belongs to them. Therefore, in a democratic way we can say Participatory Action Research is research for the community, by the community and in the community. In this research, the researcher must be aware of the feelings, attitudes and behaviour of the people and to build people's ability and potentiality in order to understand and solve the problem amicably with the help and cooperation of the people.

In this kind of research, sometime it is done by forming peer group, particularly among children, women and people with disability. The peer group is given special training in research methods by developing research tools in order to carry out field work. This kind of research is helpful in building up the community members and producing work which is well informed by them.

8.1. Role of Researcher in Participatory Action Research

Unlike in the Conventional/Traditional research, in this research, the researcher proceeds taking initiative with the group members to a particular research problem. The researcher does not go alone. The researcher ensures the participation of people group or community before starting any field work. The researcher has the responsibility to convince the participants that the information gathered will be made available to the group and ethics of inquiry will be strictly adhered while doing research.

8.2. Issues in Participatory Action Research

The researcher, however, must be aware of some issues involved in participatory action research. The following may be identified as major issues in this type of research:

a. The first issue is how to involve people to participate in the research process and decide the area of research.

b. Second, how to maintain the difference between public and private. The Participatory Action Research that concerns with public issues must not intrude private life of the community, particularly inequalities within a family. A balanced need must be maintained between community issues and private issues.
c. Third, along the way in the research process, the researcher may lose control over the direction of the project.
d. Fourth, there is always difficulty in collaboration and therefore, issues must be agreed upon and working principles agreed in advance to safeguard the interest of all.
e. Fifth, there will always be a difficulty in doing social experiment as it is complicated and involves many factors.

9. Difference between Conventional/Traditional and Participatory Action Research

The following table shows the difference between Traditional/ Conventional Research and Participatory Action Research.

Sl. No.		Conventional/ Traditional	Participatory Action
1.	Orientation/ goal	'Filling up,' in existing knowledge, developing and testing theories	Bringing about positive change among the participants
2.	Researcher's role	Primarily that of an outsider, detached, uninvolved	Primarily to bring participants in critical awareness of the situation

3.	Choice of research problem	Based upon the interest of the researcher	Based on the self-perceived needs and interest of the participants
4.	How data is gathered?	By the Researcher, instruments constructed by the Researcher for his/her purpose	Jointly by the Researcher and the Participants
5.	View of the People	Seen as objects, source of data useful for Researcher's purpose	Seen as subjects with their own concerns and priorities, treated as participants in determining their history
6.	Nature	Research-*on*-people	Research *with* people

Summary

There are two broad categories of research in social science – conventional or traditional and participatory action research. Traditional research is pure, experimental and quantitative in nature where the researcher remains detached and people or subjects are considered object of research. On the other hand, in participatory action research the researcher is one of the participants in the research process. Conventional or traditional research is research *on* people but participatory action research is research *with* people. There is difference between method and methodology, method is tool or technique process to collect data and methodology is science or study of method. In any research, the researcher needs to bring any solution or conclusion to a research problem logically. There are three types of logic or reasoning – deductive, inductive and abductive.

References

Ahuja, Ram. *Research Method.* New Delhi: Rawat Publications, 2011.

Desrochers, John. *Method of Social Analysis.* New York: Appleton-Century Company, 1941.

Dwivedi, R. S. *Methods of Behavioural Science.* Delhi: McMillan Limited, 1977.

Laws, Sophie. *Research for Development: A Practical Guide.* London: SAGE Publications Ltd., 2003.

Mabry, Hunter P. *A Manuel for Research and Writers.* Bangalore: The Board of Theological Education Senate of Serampore, 2018.

Singleton, Royce A. and Bruce Straits. *Approaches to Social Research,* Third Edition. New York: Oxford University Press, 2002.

Sjoberg, Gideon and Robert Nett. *Methodology of Social Research.* Jaipur: Rawat Publications, 2002.

Further Reading

Burns, Robert B. *Introduction to Research Methods.* London: SAGE Publications Ltd. 2000.

Ghosh, B. N. *Scientific Method and Social Research.* New Delhi: Sterling Publishers Private Limited, 1992.

Nunthura, C. "Methodological Issues in Social Research." In *Methodological Issues in Theological Research: An Exploration.* Edited by H. Vanlalauva. Kolkata: Department of Research/SATHRI, 2013.

Patton, Michael Quin, *Qualitative Research and Evaluation Method.* London: SAGE Publications, 2001.

Punch, Keith F. *Introduction to Social Research.* Los Angeles: SAGE Publications, 2007.

Whyte, William Foote, ed. *Participatory Action Research.* London: SAGE Publications, 1991.

Chapter 3

Quantitative Method and Qualitative Method in Theological Research

Introduction

In the previous chapter we have discussed two broad categories of research – Conventional/Traditional and Participatory Action research. Now the question is, how do we carry out and analyse these two categories of research in theological research? There are many methods by which we can carry out and analyse theological research. But they can be grouped in two broad categories – Quantitative Analysis (QA) Method and Qualitative Analysis (QA) Method.

1. Quantitative Method

In social science research, empirical research began some 150 years ago. With that quantitative method of research gained ascendency in empirical study. The early social scientists were impressed in the progress of natural science, because it is based on experiment and measurement. In the 1950s and 1960s quantitative research began to broaden its scope of experiment. The logic of experiment was extended first to quasi-experimental and then to non-experimental research. The development of quantitative research led to two strands, first is the comparison between group, based on experiment, t-test, and analysis of variance as its main statistical feature. The second strand was the relationship between variables, based on non-experiment reasoning, with correlation and regression as its main feature. The true experiment in quantitative method look 'downward' or 'forward,' from independent variable to dependent variable. The correlational survey looks 'upwards' or 'backwards,' from dependent variable to independent variable. There are three types of quantitative research – experimental, quasi-experimental and correlational survey.

Quantitative method of research deals with numbers. We describe data collected through research by numbers. Therefore, it is numerical in its character. The data collected are analysed and interpreted using statistical techniques, normally called SPSS (Statistical Package for the Social Sciences). The researcher turns the data into numbers through tabulation, chart, figure, index, symbols etc. The purpose of quantitative method is to draw conclusion as objective as possible. However, we must admit the fact that absolute objectivity is a myth. Nevertheless, quantitative method attempts to draw conclusion as objective as possible.

The quantitative method focusses on the aspects of social behaviour of community or group with less detail than qualitative method. It attempts to quantify the findings in numbers. In quantitative research the universe is separated in empirical components, which are called 'variables.' For example, age, sex, class, grades, colour etc. There are mainly three types of variables – independent variable and dependent variable and controlled (covariates) variable. Quantitative research is associated with the principle of 'positivism' (positivist), originally postulated by Herbert Spencer in social science.

In quantitative method there are mainly three designs – experimental design, quasi-experimental design and non-experimental design. Experimental design means the researcher follows the scientific research design that involves testing or proving the hypothesis through experimentation. Its primary focus is to find out the relation between cause and effect among variables in a controlled condition. Quasi-experimental design means that the experimental principles are applied in investigation under study, however non-experimental treatment is not controlled. Non-experimental method means there is no manipulation or changes in this type of research but rather studies the nature/phenomenon/community as it is. This method is mainly used in ethnography and anthropology.

1.1. Quantitative Method of Data Collection

In Quantitative method we collect data with the following methods:

a. Interview

We can carry out research through interview with structured, semi-structured or unstructured questionnaire. We can interview through personal meeting in face to face, through telephone or computer assisted personal interview – through emails, WhatsApp etc.

b. Questionnaire

In this method the researcher uses structured questionnaire and distribute to the people where research is conducted. If anyone is doing research with a particular church organization on a particular research problem, then the researcher will develop questions related to the research problem. The questionnaire consists of both close ended questions and open-ended questions. This method can be done through mail, email and now even through other technical means such as WhatsApp.

1.2. Strategies and Technique of Managing Quantitative Data

a. Preparation of Data for Analysis

The data collected through quantitative method have to be stored – say through hard copy or even in soft copy. Normally data storing is done through hard copy. Then it must be analysed.

1.3. Levels of Measurement

The data collected through quantitative method must be measured. There are four levels of measurement – nominal, ordinal, interval and ratio. Nominal Variables are those which have categories and can be separated them from each other just because they are different. For example – sex. It has the categories of male and female. Ordinal Variables is done by ranking of categories in hierarchical order. Internal Variables are done by distinguishing the names and can be stored the data in specified format. Ratio Variables is a type of continuous variables that has clear definition of zero, and allows for the computation of ratios, percentage and averages. Further description of these levels will be done in chapter seven.

1.4. Advantages and Disadvantages of Quantitative Method

As far as advantages are concerned, it is good for comparative analysis, there is possibility to get lots of data in a short span of time, it takes less time to respond to answer and often interesting to read. However, it also has disadvantages like – response may not be specific, questions may be misinterpreted, may not get as many responses as the researcher need, may not get the full story and depending on format may need some level of good writing skill.

2. Qualitative Method

Qualitative method of research evolved during the qualitative summer institute held in 1994 in Vail, Colorado. It is defined as the technique of gathering, analysing, interpretation and presentation of narrative. It has diverse traditions, with multiple nature of methodologies and research practices. Qualitative method is a systematic process of finding out the meaning of which people employ to make sense out of and guide their actions. The key idea of this research is to uncover, articulate and elucidate meaning. The data collected by qualitative research method is defined as empirical information about the world, however, not in the form of numbers but most of the times described through words. It does not give importance on experiment and mathematical analysis of data to come to conclusion of a particular research undertaken.

Qualitative research method encompasses mainly three aspects, such as – paradigm, approaches to data, and analysis of data. The main paradigms in qualitative research are positivism, postpositivism, critical theory and constructivism. In data collection process both ethical question and professionalism are involved. The researcher has to maintain both of these aspects in research process to be holistic and comprehensive in its complex nature. Through the analysis of data, which is also known as "thick description," the researcher attempts to bring out interpretation from multiple perspectives.

Qualitative research is carried out in real human life situation. The objective of this method is to describe and illuminate people's behaviour and thoughts through their real and natural social interactions. Through analysis it tries to derive meanings from people themselves, so it is eclectic in nature.

2.1. Data Collection Procedure in Qualitative Method

In qualitative method, data is collected by different means. It can be done through *In-depth Interviewing.* It can be done in following ways – first by one-to-one interview where each of the respondents is questioned at a length about particular issue, experience or event. The second, by *group discussion* on a particular issue, experience or event by which the group will give to a common view regarding the research issue. In depth one-to-one interview need not be structured but can be done through open-ended questions. It uses flexible questions. Interview is held with the participants of a particular group, say – youth, adult, scientists etc. The third method is, it is done through *Focus Group*. Finally, it is done through *ethnography* and *observation.* Ethnography is a study on particular ethnic group, culture and customs. And this is done through observation.

Whether it is focus group or one-to-one interview, the researcher must decide how to record the data. It can be done through notebook or by recording. Now a days it also can be done by video recording with due permission from the interviewee. In both approaches there are practical problems. In recording, whether audio or video, the interviewee may become nervous and may not be able to answer the question properly. Then in taking note the interviewer has to make quick decision which one to note because the researcher cannot make the interviewee wait for next question. The strategy of *managing field note* also can be done in qualitative research. Managing field note is done writing down the minute of the meeting, recording the messages of the telephone or distributing paper to pen down their ideas. The purpose of note taking is to capture the essence of what we observe and record it for future, because a level of accuracy is important in research.

2.2. Three Kinds of Qualitative Data

There are mainly three kinds of qualitative data – interview, observation and documents:

a. Interview: Interview is done through open ended questions. Open ended questions yield in depth responses about people's experiences, perceptions, opinion, feelings, and knowledge. It consists of verbatim quotations with sufficient context.
b. Observation: Observation involves fieldwork description of activities, behaviours, actions, conversations, interpersonal interactions, organizational and community processes or any other aspect of observable human experiences. Data consists of field notes, rich and detailed description, including context within which the observations were made.
c. Documents: Documents consist of written materials and other documents from organizational, clinical, or programme reports, memoranda and correspondence, official publications and reports, personal diaries, artistic works, photographs, and memorabilia. It consists of response to open ended survey and documents recorded and preserved by experts.

2.3. Strategies and Techniques for Managing Qualitative Data

The word 'strategy' comes from Greek *Strategos*, which means "thinking and action of a general." The term is attached to Alexander, the great. Alexander defeated Persian king of kings

Darius III, who had 250,000 army personals with the army of 50,000. His victory is attributed to his strategic plan of the war, where he studied the anthropology, worldview and culture of the enemy to develop a strategic plan to defeat. In social research strategy is to gain psychological, sociological and anthropological insights of people group, community, culture etc.

2.4. Design Strategies for Qualitative Inquiry

There are certain designs to carry out qualitative inquiry as follows:

a. Naturalistic Inquiry

Qualitative research designs are naturalistic in nature to the extent that the research is carried out in the real-world settings and the researcher does not attempt to manipulate the phenomena of the interest of the group, community and events and programmes and the relationships and interactions.

b. Emergent Design Flexibility

In qualitative research naturalistic and pragmatic consideration is paramount. It is open and pragmatic that include openness, tolerance and trust. In the process of research, if there is a need to change the method, strategy and plan, it is open to do so.

c. Purposeful Samplings

Qualitative research typically focusses on relatively small samples compared to quantitative research. Qualitative research differs from quantitative in terms of strategy, logic and purposes. Quantitative method depends on larger samples, selected randomly in order to generalize with confidence from the sample to the population that it represents.

2.5. Data Collection and Fieldwork Strategies

Patton (2002) offers the following methods of data collection and field work strategies for qualitative research.

a. Qualitative Data

In qualitative research data is collected mainly through a detailed observation with thick description by conducting in depth interview that capture direct questions about people's perspectives and experiences. It is done through careful case study and document review.

b. Direct Personal Experience and Engagement: Going into the Field

In the qualitative research, the researcher has direct contact with people, situation and phenomenon under study. In this research, researcher's personal experience and insights are very important in the process of inquiry for critical reflection. Qualitative inquiry involves going into the field – into the real world of programmes, organizations, community and people group under study. It is to get close enough to the people and circumstances by immersing oneself naturally to capture the complexities involved in the problem/issue under study. Going to the field and having personal contact with the people under study is not only legitimate way to understand human behaviour but necessary and desirable for face to face in depth interview.

c. Empathy Neutrality and Mindfulness

The qualitative interviewing is conducted without judgement with vicarious understanding by showing openness, sensitivity, respect, awareness, and responsiveness. Interview is carried out with mindfulness and understanding. However, according to Patton, in any research there is no universal perception that can capture the range of possibilities for any given research because it will depend on the situation, the nature of inquiry and the perspective of the researcher. Therefore, strategically he offers middle ground what he calls "empathic neutrality" as a point of departure between subjectivity and objectivity. In research project the terms *objectivity* and *subjectivity* have become loaded with negative connotation. The empathic neutrality attempts to strike a balance between objectivity and subjectivity.

d. Dynamic System/Development Perspective

Being mindful and attentive to system and situation dynamics is very necessary in qualitative research. A researcher must be mindful whether the focus is on an individual, an organization, a community or on an entire culture is important. The dynamics of situation keeps on changing. Today's findings for solution of a particular issue or problem would become obsolete and irrelevant in the next 5 to 10 years of time (except may be in some historical studies). Therefore, the researcher should be mindful of the fast and ever-changing world. In social science no researcher should absolutize and essentialize his/her findings. Naturalistic or qualitative inquiry try not to control, limit or draw to a foreclosure but expect change and new horizon of meaning with vitality and vigour.

2.6. Strategies of Analysis

a. Unique Case Orientation

The researcher needs to consider each case in a unique way. Each case is unique and special. Therefore, the researcher needs to approach each case with respect and be true to each individual case. He/she needs to capture entire process of inquiry and make cross-analysis for quality research.

b. Inductive Analysis and Creative Synthesis

The researcher needs to immerse on the issue or events in order to gain detail and specific data so that he/she can discover important patterns, themes, interrelationship by exploring, confirming, and analysing rather than rules and end with creative synthesis.

c. Holistic Perspective

Approach in qualitative research is holistic or what we call Gestaltic. It is more than sum of its parts. The issue or problem is as a complex phenomenon interrelated and interconnected with other issues. So, the issue or problem is dealt from different angles and perspective to have a holistic understanding without which dynamics cannot be treated meaningfully to draw discrete variables and cause-effect relationship.

d. Context Sensitivity

In any research context is inevitable. Context can be historical, social, and temporal. A careful study of context about events, phenomenon, group, community or organizations is very crucial in qualitative research. There cannot be text without context. Context can be dubious but still then proper analysis is important for possibility or meaningful generalization across time and space. It helps in emphasizing careful comparative case analysis by extrapolating possible transferability and adaptation in new settings.

e. Voice, Presence and Reflexibility

In qualitative research, the researcher owns and becomes reflective about his/her own voice and perspective. He/she does not remain detached and in unreflective mode. He/she tries to convey credible voice, authenticity, and trustworthy. In this research, the researcher moves from third person (singular/plural) to first person (singular/plural). Using first person is considered unacademic in quantitative research but it is quite acceptable in qualitative research. As Patton rightly says, complete objectivity is impossible but again pure subjectivity undermines credibility. Therefore, the researcher must attempt to strike a balance by understanding world authentically with all its complexity while attempting to be self-analytical, politically aware and reflexive consciousness. Self-reflexivity consists of dynamic feedback loop whereby one's own findings are brought into reflective awareness. For the research on subaltern issues, we can also add "agency." This is mainly, postcolonial, postmodern and feminist perspective, which readily applies in the study of Tribals, Adivasis, Women and Dalits.

2.7. Advantages and Disadvantages of Qualitative Method

There are a number of advantages in qualitative method. It helps to develop a bigger picture. There is good community participation. It helps in developing ideas and sharing talents. It enables to get information from number of individuals. However, there are also disadvantages in this method. It can be time consuming. It might be difficult to arrange the time for interview, particularly in focus group interview. In certain cases, participants may have to be paid as an incentive for attending in group discussion or focus group. There could be language problem also. There may be need of an interpreter. There could arise difficulties in organizing and analysing the information.

2.8. Difference between Qualitative and Quantitative Analysis Method

Attribute	Qualitative	Quantitative
Analytical Objective	Focus on to describe individual experiences and beliefs	Focus on to decide the characteristics of population
Types of questions asked	Open ended questions	Close ended questions
Forms of data collection	Descriptive data- focus group, in depth interview	Numerical data- survey, structured interview and observation
Degree of flexibility	Participants response affect how and which question researcher ask next – subjective	Participants response do not influence or determine how and which question to ask – objective

2.9. Combining Quantitative and Qualitative Methods: Mixed Method

The combination of quantitative and qualitative methods, which is also normally called "mixed method" is described by various names, such as – *third path* (Conrad and Taylor, 2004), *third research paradigm* (Johnson and Onwuegbuzie, 2004), *third methodological movement* (Teddlie and Tashakkori, 2003) and *third research community*. Tashakkori and Creswell define mixed method as a "research in which the investigator collects and analyse data, integrates findings, and draws inferences from both qualitative and quantitative approaches and methods in a single study or program."

While quantitative research is based on numerical data and analysis within the framework of positivists/ postpositivist paradigm, qualitative method works within the framework that emphasizes on narrative data and analysis in constructivism paradigm. But mixed method works within the framework of both numerical data and narrative based on pragmatist paradigm. In theological education, particularly in Christian ministry the researcher has to use both qualitative and qualitative approaches even in rudimentary level.

For the sake of study, we may differentiate these quantitative and qualitative methods of research. But none of them can make an exclusive claim. For a comprehensive research we may have to use both methods. Therefore, now a day both methods are used together in social science research – what we call 'mixed-method.' All methods have their own strengths and weaknesses. We can bring these methods together in three ways: Qualitative method could be used to explore a particular topic to set for quantitative research. Conversely, we can start with quantitative method in order to collect sample and to establish the broad contour of the field and then move to qualitative method. We can use both methods together by engaging in a qualitative study which uses the quantitative data to locate the result in a broader context.

a. Data Analysis and Interpretation in Mixed Method

William H. Greene points out four types of data analysis and interpretation in mixed method as follows:

i. *Triangulation:* It means using two points and their angles to determine the third point as mixed method looks for compatibility between different viewpoints. There are four points in triangulations, such as – triangulation of data, of investigators, of theory and methodological triangulation.

ii. *Complementarity:* It means the purpose of the researcher in mixed method is to seek elaboration, illustration, enhancement, clarification of the findings from both qualitative and quantitative standpoints that complements each other.

iii. *Development:* It means one analytical strand would help to inform the other analytical strand. For example, taking interview on the basis of observational data.

iv. *Initiation:* It means the researcher looking into paradox and contradiction emerging out of findings when two strands are compared. For example, contradiction between questionnaire and interview. Such contradiction might lead to more questions that the researcher has to initiate.

v. *Expansion:* It means that in the process, the researcher might attempt to expand the breadth and range of investigation in different phases, when necessity arises.

Summary

There are mainly two kinds of method of analysis – Quantitative Analysis (QA) and Qualitative Analysis (QA). Quantitative method is numerical and deals with number. In quantitative method, data are collected through interview and questionnaire. Questionnaire contain close-ended questions and open-ended questions. The purpose of quantitative method is to draw conclusion of a research problem as objectively as possible. There are three kinds of research designs in quantitative research – experimental design, quasi-experimental design and non-experimental design.

Qualitative method is a systematic process of finding out the meaning of which people employ to make sense out of and guide their action. The key idea of qualitative method is to uncover, articulate, and elucidate meaning. In qualitative method both ethical question and professionalism are involved. In qualitative method data are collected mainly through interview, focus group, case study, and group discussion. Interview method consists of structured, semi structured and unstructured questions. Now a day, both quantitative and qualitative methods are increasingly used in social research, which is called "mixed method."

References

Best, John W. and James V. Kahn. *Research in Education.* New Delhi: PHI Learning Private Ltd., 2012.

Charles, Teddlie and Abbas Tashakkori. *Foundations of Mixed Method Research.* New Delhi: SAGE Publications, 2009.

Creswell, John W. *Qualitative Inquiry and Research Design.* New Delhi: SAGE Publications, 1998.

Desai, Vandana and Robert B. Potter. *Doing Development Research.* New Delhi: Vistar Publications, 2006.

Ghosh, B. N. *Scientific Method and Social Research.* New Delhi: Sterling Publishers Pvt. Ltd., 2011.

Henn, Matt, Mark Weinstein and Nick Ford. *A Short Introduction to Social Research.* New Delhi: Vistar Publication, 2006.

McLeod, John. *Practitioner Research in Counselling.* London: SAGE Publications Ltd., 1999.

Silver, David. *Interpreting Qualitative Data.* London: SAGE Publications, 1993.

Patton, Michael Quinn. *Qualitative Research & Evaluation Method,* 3rd Edition. Thousand Oakes; London; New Delhi: Sage Publications, 2002.

Punch, Keith F. *Introduction to Social Research: Quantitative and Qualitative Approaches,* Second Edition. Los Angeles; London; New Delhi; Singapore: SAGE Publications, 2005.

Chapter 4

Steps in Research Process

Introduction

Research means 'to investigate thoroughly' on something. It is a systematic study of materials and sources in order to establish fact to reach to new conclusion. To carry out any research systematically there are steps which we must follow, otherwise we will end up in confusion and chaos. Any researcher must follow these steps systematically. Some of them may overlap but we must try to follow sequentially. The following are the steps in social research:

1. Steps in the Research Process

1.1. Selection of the Subject Area

The first step the researcher has to take is selection of research area. A researcher may encounter many areas where he/she feels the need of research. But the researcher must be able to select an area by his/her own judgement that is pertaining to society, academic field or any other field of discipline that the researcher is in. Sometime the decision of selection may be influenced by subjective factors. But the subjective proclivity is insufficient, therefore, the researcher must include community in the process of selection of research area.

1.2. Identification of Research Problem

Selection of research area is not sufficient. In a given research area there may be many problems and issues. The researcher must narrow down the area within a particular problem. Out of that research problem, the researcher must develop research questions. The identification of research problem could be from his/her interest or could be from agency. The identification of problem could be completely new one or based on existing knowledge. The identification of problem could be either in the quest of some intellectual pursuit or for some practical concern in order to find practical solution to the problem. Or it could be evaluation of existing knowledge in finding new facts for planning and policy making.

1.3. Extensive Literature Survey

Once the problem research is identified an extensive survey of literature has to be done. This step will depend upon the nature and extend of the research. Literature would include books, journals, published and unpublished materials, biographies and even archives. In certain research, conference proceedings would also be included. At the same time care must be taken not to survey unnecessary literature. It should be remembered once source will lead to another. Now a day the researcher can also avail lots of sources through internet.

1.4. Formulation of Hypothesis

Once extensive literature survey is done the researcher will have some idea to proceed to formulate tentative solution or answer to the research problem. This proposal to solution is called 'hypothesis.' Hypothesis is a compound of two words – 'hypo' and 'thesis,' where hypo literally means under or below and thesis means theory or rational viewpoint. Therefore, hypothesis would mean a theory which is not fully reasoned. It is a theory entertained in order to study the facts and examine the validity of the theory. A hypothesis is a well stated and framed statement for what we are looking to investigate. When facts are assembled, ordered, and seen in relationships, they constitute a theory. A theory is not speculation, but built upon facts. Now, various facts in a theory may be analysed, and relationships established other than those stated in the theory can be deduced. At this point there is no knowledge as to whether such deductions are correct or incorrect. The formulation of the deduction, however, constitute a hypothesis, if verified, it becomes part of the future theoretical construction. Sometime a researcher may need to develop working hypothesis.

1.5. Research Design

Designing a research is a step, where the researcher will decide how to carry out the research project. Before launching any action, the researcher must decide the design. There are a number of research designs at the disposal of social science research. Depending on the nature of the research project, one may have to adopt more than one research design. Researcher must be careful that he/she does not need to take detour, because it will cost time, energy and money. If a team is involved in the research, the team members may lose interest and motivation.

1.6. Sample Design

If the research project involves breadth and length, the researcher may have to make sample. The process of collection of data from population is known as sample. Therefore, sample design is a plan of collection of samples from the universe. It is decided in advance before data collection. The researcher has the freedom to choose the sample design. In simple term, sampling means that in any research we need to have "representation' of the target people. To be representative means to provide 'maximization' of certain characteristics of the target people under study. For example, to investigate the effectiveness of curriculum of the Senate of Serampore college (University) for Bachelor of Divinity degree, there has to be *maximum* representation of students from different theological colleges and seminaries. There are two classes of samplings, *probability sampling* and *nonprobability sampling.* Probability sampling is scientifically acceptable, although it is not always feasible and economical for every research. In probability sampling population are randomly selected and in nonprobability sampling the chances of any case are not known because cases are randomly selected. In probability sampling random selection is done, which is normally called *random sampling.* Again, probability sampling also can be done in stratified manner, which is called *stratified sampling.* Stratified sampling simply means that if the population is too vast then it is subdivided in two or more exclusive segments, called *strata.* In certain research both random sampling and stratified sampling may not be adequate when population is too large. In that case *cluster sampling* will be required. In cluster sampling population is broken down into groups, called cluster.

On the other, nonprobability sampling refers to the process of case selection other than random selection. However, nonprobability sampling has two basic weaknesses, first, it does not control investigator's bias in the selection unit, second, its pattern of variable cannot be predicted, which makes evaluation of sampling difficult to find out error or wrong findings. That said, sometime nonprobability sampling is more predictable than probability sampling.

Therefore, as far as possible in a given research the researcher needs to keep mind open for both these samplings.

1.7. Data Collection

Data collection is a process by which relevant information are collected from various sources. The data collection process can be divided into two categories – method of primary source data collection and secondary source of data collection. Again, primary source data collection can be divided into two groups – quantitative and qualitative, which we have discussed already in the previous chapter. Secondary source of data collection is done through already available sources, say – the data which already been collected and analysed by someone else. Secondary data could be either published or unpublished. In whatever way, due acknowledgement is a must.

1.8. Execution of the Research Project

After the collection of required data, now the researcher can move to real execution of the project. By now the researcher is assumed to have enough resources at his/her disposal. This step is very important. It has to be done systematically, considering time factor, expenses and energy. If the execution of research is correct and in right direction, collected data would be adequate and dependable. Here the researcher must ensure that the survey is under statistical control, that is collected information agrees with the pre-defined standard of accuracy.

1.9. Analysis of Data

Once execution of the research starts, then the next step is to analyse the data. This is normally done through the SPSS in quantitative research. The data analysis is done through tables, charts, diagram, ratio and indexes. It means the application of statistical technique. We must remember the fact that all data may not be amenable to quantitative data analysis. Here the role of mixed-method comes into play. An alternative approach may have to be taken. But the analysis of raw data has to start.

1.10. Testing of Hypothesis

In actual social science research, testing of hypothesis is required. The main purpose of testing hypothesis is to determine the possibility supported by fact. After analysing the data, the researcher is in a position to test the hypothesis. The purpose is to test whether the facts support the hypothesis or they happen to be contrary. This question should be answered while testing hypothesis. If the facts and the hypothesis do not align then the researcher may have to take detour or reworked the hypothesis. If the researcher had no hypothesis to begin with then the generalization established on the basis of data may be stated as hypothesis to be tested. In theological research in some disciplines, such as – theology, history and biblical studies, hypothesis is not compulsory.

1.11. Generalization and Interpretation

After testing hypothesis, the researcher can make generalization that will construed to be real value of research. In social science, it is possible only when hypothesis testing is done. But if the researcher does not have hypothesis, then he/she may seek to interpret the findings. He/she can explain the findings on the basis of theoretical framework, which may probably raise some new questions for further researches. In theological research many disciplines do not attach to hypothesis.

1.12. Reporting the Research

This step may not take place in many researches, particularly in a study like theology. But in social science research this is an integral part of the steps of research. This is the final step in research project. The writing of research has to be precise, accurate and attractive. It is a technical task. Command and grasp of language will beautify the report. It does not demand skill but demands effort, patience and penetration of overall approach of the problem and data analysis. Once the report is accepted by the panel of experts then only the actual writing can start in social science research.

Summary

Any research has to be done systematically and step by step. The researcher needs to follow these steps one after another. There are twelve steps a researcher needs to follow, first - selection of research area, second - identification of research problem, third - extensive literature survey, fourth - formulation of hypothesis, fifth - research design, sixth - sample design, seventh - data collection, eight – execution of research project, ninth - analysis of data, tenth - testing of hypothesis, eleventh - generalization and interpretation and twelfth - reporting the research. In theological research the last step need not be necessary.

References

Babu, Ramesh G. *Research Methodology in Social Science.* New Delhi: Concept Publishing Company, 2008.

Bryman, Alan. *Social Research Method.* New York: Oxford University Press, 2012.

Kothari, C. R. *Research Methodology: Methods and Techniques.* New Delhi: New Age International (P) Limited Publishers, 1985.

Lodico, Marguerite G. *Methods in Educational Research – From Theory to Practice.* San Francisco: Josey Bass, A Wiley Imprint, 2006.

Mabry, Hunter P. *A Manuel of Researcher and Writers.* Bangalore: BTESS, 2018.

Sharma, P. K. *Research Methodology.* New Delhi: Maxford Books, 2013.

Sing, Yogesh Kumar. *Fundamentals of Research Methodology and Statistics.* New Delhi: New Age International (P) Limited Publisher, 2006.

Singleton, Royce A. Jr. and Bruce A. Straits. *Approaches to Social Research,* Third Edition. New York, Oxford: Oxford University Press, 1999.

Vanit, Nalwa. *The ABC of Research for Behaviour and Social Science.* New Delhi: Wiley Eastern Limited, 1992.

Chapter 5

Types of Research and Research Design

Introduction

For any research project a good research design is inevitable, so also in any theological research project. The term 'design' means 'drawing,' or an 'outline' or 'planning' or 'arranging' something in details. It is a process on which research will move. It helps in decision making along the way in research. A research design is a logical and systematic plan for directing research project. It specifies the objective, methodology and technique of study. Research design depends on the type of research chosen for a particular research work.

1. Definitions

F. N. Kerlinger cited by Devendra Thakur defines, "Research design is the plan, structure, and strategy of investigation conceived so as to obtain answers to research questions and to control variance." Martin Bulmer cited by Ram Ahuja defines, "Research design is the specification of the problem, conceptual definition, derivation of hypothesis to test, and defining of population to be studied."

Punch defines research design as "it means all the issues involved in planning and executing a research project – from identifying the problem through reporting and publishing the results." This is in general sense. In specific sense, "the design of a study [research] refers to the way a research guards against, and tries to rule out, alternative interpretation of research." The research design is the basic plan for a piece of research, and includes four main ideas – the first is strategy, the second is conceptual framework and the third is the question of who or what will be studied. The fourth concerns the tools and procedures to be used for collecting and analysing empirical materials. Therefore, research design deals with four main questions. First, what strategy to follow. The centre of research design is the logic or rational to follow in the research project. The reasoning or the set of ideas is the main intention by which the researcher wants to proceed his/her research project. The second concern is framework, both theoretical and conceptual depending on the nature of study. The third question or concern is sampling for the research. It is mainly in quantitative and qualitative studies. The general question the researcher needs to ask is "Who or What will be studied?" And the fourth concern is how data will be collected. It is about tools and procedures to be followed in data collection process and analysis, especially in quantitative research.

The plan in the research design include everything to be done by the investigator in research procedure that is from writing the hypothesis, defining hypothesis operationally and collecting data to final analysis of data. The term structure means specifically the outline of the specific research project. The term strategy refers to methods to be used to gather and analyse data.

2. Functions/Goals of Research Design

a. Research Design provides blue print to the researcher to carry out any given research. Just as to build a house, blue print is required for the builder in the same way research design provides blue print to the researcher.

b. It limits the boundaries of research activity. Without blue print the researcher will wander around and will not be able to meet any conclusion. It helps to focus in determining causes out of many probable causes.

c. It enables investigator to anticipate potential problems. In the process of research, the researcher studies available literatures which might lead to new/alternative approaches.

Berger et.al. (1989) provide the following goals/function of research design:

a. It provides right direction to the researcher as to how to proceed in research investigation that enables to reduce time and cost.

b. It provides systematic approach in the execution of research in right sequence.

c. It helps in coordination and effective organization.

d. It helps in proper utilization of resources and to avoid errors and bias.

e. When investigators are employed, it enables the researcher to control the operation of investigation.

Manheim (1977) provides five goals of research design as follows:

a. It helps to amass more evidence to support given hypothesis and eliminate alternative hypothesis.

b. It helps, as far as possible to make study worth replicable, which can be done by avoiding situations and procedures that are clearly unique.
c. It helps to associate variables with another and gives propositions in such a way that they become easy to determine.
d. It helps to determine whether or not pilot study is necessary for future plan.
e. It helps in planning technique in the collection process of data by avoiding useless and irrelevant facts, thus it reduces time and money.

In designing research, the researcher needs to keep in mind that no single method is adequate enough to find solution to a particular problem. Therefore, based on the nature of investigation, the researcher may have to employ more than one or two methods, because no method is perfect for data collection. This will give the researcher confidence and reliability in his/her findings. Generally, research is focussed mainly on two variables – independent variable and dependent variable. In certain researches we need to use multiple variables, which is called multivariate analysis. For example, spiritual decline of Christian youth cannot be explained with just one variable. There can be many variables, such as – lack of proper teaching on the part of the church, negligence of parents, peer influence and influence of social media and globalization. Explaining dependent variable based on only one independent variable will not suffice to draw logical conclusion.

3. The Purpose of Research Design

There are basically two purposes of research design:

a. It is to provide answers to reach a problem as valid, objective, accurate, and economically viable as possible.

b. It is to bring empirical evidence to bear on the research problem by controlling variance. There are three ways as to how to control variance. It can be done 1) by maximizing systematic variance 2) by controlling or eliminating extraneous variance and 3) minimizing error variance.

4. Factors of Research Design

The following are some factors of research design:

a. The researcher should know the different points of data collection. He/she should know whether the data should be collected at one point of time or in different stages. For example, study on the rehabilitation of programme of drug addict. The study of time period should be three months, six months, one year or two year etc.

b. Researcher should know the many research situations of say – church, association, diocese, age groups, organization etc.

c. The researcher should ensure whether changes have to be made along the way in research process. Now this may not be possible in theological research unless hypothesis does not guarantee any logical conclusion. However, in social science option for changes must be kept wide open.

d. In some research comparative study may be required. For example, study on the impact of social media on youth. The impact of social media on youth may differ from urban to rural.

e. The researcher should make it clear whether the research design is descriptive, exploratory or explanatory, pure or applied.

5. Requirements for Good Research Design

To ascertain a good research design, the following characteristics may be noted:

a. Nature and scope of the problem must be stated clearly, or it must be well defined and formulated.
b. If any hypothesis to be tested, it must be clearly formulated.
c. The research design must adequately answer the research questions and test the hypothesis.
d. Relevant variables must be clearly identified and operationalized. Adequate methods of collecting the information and methods of logically deriving conclusion must be developed.
e. The research design must be structured in a manner that fulfills the need of internal and external validity.
f. Researcher should know how many research situations, i.e., individuals, groups, communities; organizations, etc. will be of his/her interest and how are these varied situations to be interrelated.
g. The researcher should select appropriately the types of research, i.e., descriptive, exploratory and experimental design.

6. Advantages of Research Design

There are various advantages in designing research project, such as follows:

a. In helps in conducting research in scientific manner since it is directed by precise guidelines that reduces inaccuracies.
b. It minimizes time, money and energy.
c. It helps in getting optimum reliability.

d. It helps in drawing reliable conclusion based on proper hypotheses/theories.

7. Types of Research and Research Design

In what follows different types of research and research designs are discussed together. Any research work has the common purpose of finding answers to meaningful questions. Each of these research designs has its own specific purpose. The research design may vary from each other in their specific purpose.

7.1. Exploratory Research Design

This research design is applied when the researcher does not have acquaintance with the problem or the community, where he/she conducting research. When a new area or field of research is undertaken, this research design is employed. The purpose of this research design is to achieve new insights into the problem or the community. The major emphasis is on the discovery of ideas and insights. It is a new venture into certain problem or community. As this is a new venture, the researchers have to devise their own guide and schemes of classification. In this research design the following methods are used:

a. Literature Survey

In this research method an extensive literature survey has to be done on the given research area, on which hypothesis has not been formulated yet. Extensive literature review has to be done on the available materials in order to develop hypothesis. This research can be an incipient research launching on virgin field.

b. Experience

In exploratory research experience counts. The researcher may not have experience with the given field of research. But he/she must count the practical experiences of the people, where research is conducted. To explore certain problem, mere statistical information is not enough. Therefore, the researcher must be able to select best informants who can provide genuine and authentic information. Selecting informants has to be done carefully and strategically so that he/she can find experienced and informative people. In certain cases, elders of the community can be best informants.

c. Insights Stimulating Experiences

It is not always easy to find experienced informants to collect information and formulate hypothesis. In that case few selected individuals will be helpful and fruitful. Before carrying out investigation on the problem with the entire community, the researcher will study the people selected for investigation and from there he/she will proceed. In this respect the researcher first should seek to acquire greater knowledge about the problem rather than testing of hypothesis. For such method the researcher must have integrative power to combine diverse pieces of information for unified interpretation. In a sense it amounts to pilot project or micro research.

7.2. Descriptive Research Design

In the descriptive research design, the researcher aims to gain accurate description of the individual, community, institution, or events in such a way that there is minimum bias but maximum reliability. This descriptive research design is used primarily in ethnography. The descriptive research must be designed carefully and plan properly in order to achieve its aims and objectives to obtain complete and accurate information. A descriptive study describes and interprets what it is, as it occurs with conditions or relationship that exists, opinions that are held, processes that are going on, effects that are evident, or trends that are developing. It is used in a phenomenological approach. This is again done in phenomenological and ethnographic studies. And it is primarily concerned with the present, although it often considers past events and anticipate for future influences. In descriptive research design, normally both qualitative and quantitative methods are used. The descriptive research design also follows the research steps that we have discussed in the previous chapter, such as – formulation of objective, designing methods, data collection, selecting sample, collecting information, processing and analysing data, and reporting the findings. The main requisite in descriptive research design is also to clearly and specifically state the purpose, goals and objectives of the investigation.

This type of research design describes social situations, social events, social system, social structure etc. It does describe as it is the social events take place. It describes social system and social structure of a community/society how they occur and function. For example, women ordination in the church. The researcher collects the number of ordained women from various denominations. The researcher shows how the ordination of women is increasing in the churches. Another example could be women participation in politics in India. The researcher will take a period of years for his/her study to see the increase or decrease of women participation in politics.

7.3. Experimental Research Design

The experimental research design is to investigate the relationship between two or more factors. This research design is deliberate and purposive. This research design is applied in education and medical sciences. During the COVID-19 pandemic, experimental research was done to develop vaccine and to determine its efficacy. Experiments are to discover cause and effect of certain factors. This research design is carried out among children to formulate aims and objectives, methods and contents of education. Experimental research deals with three types of variables – dependent, independent and controlled. Variables are the conditions or characteristics that the experimenter manipulates, controls or observe. The factors which affect another variable and whose affect is under study is known as independent variable. On the other hand, the dependent variables are those characteristics of behaviour, which are influenced by the first group of factors.

The purpose of experimental research is to test causal hypothesis which is highly structured. It is to show that an independent variable causes change in the dependent variables (in case of COVID-19, physicians and patients). The primary objective of experiment is to bring out functional relationship among phenomena under controlled conditions. It attempts to give a precise answer to a precise question. The concern is to discover what leads to what.

7.4. Field Research Design

Field research design involves direct study of field situation. It is essentially a matter of immersing oneself in naturally occurring set of events in order to gain first-hand knowledge of any problem. It permits introduction of controls into data collection. There is difference between field study method and survey method. Survey method has greater scope than field research but field research method has greater depth. Survey method is representative in the nature of the known universe but field study may or may not involve in sampling. The field research method is concerned with a thorough account of the research process but survey method is concerned with the distribution of social variables in the larger group. In the field study method, we concentrate our research on a single community or tribe, but survey method more than one community or group. Sometime the whole community may be taken into consideration in survey research. It becomes more representative. The field study method provides a more detailed and more natural picture of social relationship. For example, survey method used in the research on family planning in India, composed of rural, urban, Hindu, Muslim, and Christian. But field study method may consider only one village or community.

7.5. Explanatory or Causal Research Design

This research design explains the causes of social phenomena or problems under study. The explanatory research aims to establish the relationship between variables, how one is the cause of another or how and when one variable occurs the other will also occur. It explains the relationship of one event to the other. For example, how and why communal riot takes place in India. There may be many variables connected to riot.

7.6. Survey Method Research Design

The word "survey" is derived from the words "sue" or "sor" and "veer" or "veair," which means "over" and "see." In simple term it is "overseeing" of an issue or problem. It is to take over something from a high place. Although the term is used in direct observation of something through questionnaire, it is also now a days used in the investigation of published work.

a. Some Definitions

The followings are some definitions cited by Thakur:

i. *Herman N. Morse*: The survey is in briefly a method of analysis in scientific and orderly form for defined purpose of a given social situation or problem.

ii. *Mark Abram*: A social Survey is a process by which quantitative facts are collected about social aspects of a community's composition and activities.

iii. *A. F. Wells:* A Social Survey is fact-finding study dealing with working-class poverty and with the nature and problems of community.

b. Characteristics of Survey Research

i. Social survey is confined with immediate problem of society or community/church. For example, delinquency and drug abuse among the youth, or crime or poverty of a community.

ii. Its geographical area is limited and localized.

iii. Its purpose is to prepare constructive programme through social research to deal with an issue/problem or address the immediate problem/issue.

iv. Its findings may lead to further social research and formulation of hypothesis.

In this method a systematic and comprehensive study is done on a community, organization, group etc. Survey method involves administration of questionnaire or interview to a large group of people. It aims to analyse the social problem and try to present recommendations to address a particular issue or problem. Its purpose is to describe the frequency of certain characteristics among a group or population. For example, poverty in India or violence against women in India.

c. Some Specific Purpose of Social Survey

i. Its purpose is mainly to provide some information on an issue or problem.
ii. It is to provide descriptive analysis of a phenomenon related with social condition, relationship and behaviour.
iii. Its purpose is to explain an issue/problem at theoretical level and to test hypothesis.

7.7. Evaluation Research Design

This research is generally conducted by sociologists, psychologist, economists, social workers, educationists etc. It can be used in theological education also. This research can be used in the evaluation of curriculum of any theological college or seminary. It can be used in the evaluation of an organization and its effectiveness and to assess its existing policies, implementation of programmes, proper utilization of fund etc.

Sarantakos (1998) offers the followings goals for evaluation research:

a) To discover gaps in research. b). to investigate alternatives to meet the unmet needs. c) to predict whether a planned programme will be successful. d) to assess the effectiveness of the programme. e) to establish whether programme is cost effective and whether benefit outweigh the cost. f) to identify the ways to improve the effectiveness of research.

We can add more types of research design, such as, diagnostic and correlational research design. Diagnostic research design looks to evaluate the underlying causes of a specific topic or phenomenon. This design helps one learn more about the factors that create troublesome situation. The correlational research design is non-experimental. It is a technique that helps to establish a relationship between two closely connected variables. This type of research requires two different groups. There is no prior assumption while evaluating a relationship between two different variables. Statistical analysis technique is used to calculate the relationship between the two variables.

Summary

For a successful research project, a relevant and appropriate research design is inevitable. Research design depends on the types and nature of research. In this chapter, few research designs discussed are: exploratory research design, descriptive research design, experimental research design, field research design, field study research design, explanatory research design, survey research design and evaluation research design.

References

Ahuja, Ram. *Research Methods.* New Delhi: Rawat Publications, 2018.

Evans, Annabel Ness and Bryan J. Rooney. *Methods in Psychological Research.* New Delhi: SAGE Publications, 2008.

Good, Carter V, A. R. Barr and Douglas E. Scathes. *Methodology of Educational Research.* New Delhi: Appleton-Century Company, 1941.

Kothari, C. R. *Research Methodology: Methods and Techniques.* New Delhi: Viswa Prakashan, 1990.

Nakkiran, S. and G. Ramesh. *Research Methods in Rural Development.* New Delhi: Deep Publications Pvt. Ltd, 2009.

Saravanavel, P. *Research Methodology.* Allahabad: Kitab Mahal, 2011.

Thakur, Devendra. *Research Methodology in Social Science.* New Delhi: Deep and Deep Publications, Pvt. Ltd, 2008.

Punch, Keith F. *Introduction to Social Research: Quantitative and Qualitative Approaches,* Second Edition. Los Angeles; London; New Delhi; Singapore: SAGE Publications, 2005.

Chapter 6

Selection and Formulation of Research Problem

Introduction

Selection and formulation of research problem is another very important aspect in research project. It can be done even before deciding research design. In our discussion on the steps of research, we have come across that selection of research problem is the second step in overall research project. It was also pointed out that selection of research area (the first step) is not enough, but we have to narrow it down to research problem. Again, we need to spell out that research problem to a specific topic.

A research problem is a clear and definite expression of an area of concern, a condition to be improved upon, a difficulty to be eliminated, or a troubling question that has to be addressed. In order to do that researcher needs to select a particular topic depending on his/her ability, available resources and time and so on. After selecting the problem, the researcher has to formulate the topic. While formulating the topic, the difficulties and problems must be looked into, whether theoretical or practical. Just like asking research questions is important, formulation of research problem is more important than solution, because, without problem there is no solution and without question there is no answer. Or you cannot expect answer.

1. Selection of Research Topic

Once research problem is identified, it has to be narrowed down to a topic. You express the research problem with precise form and choice of words. For example, if your research area is on social issues among adolescents (that is your research area), then you want to deal on social media (your research problem), then further you narrow down your research problem to a specific topic, say, "The Impact of Social Media among the Adolescents in Dimapur, Nagaland" (your research topic). Your research topic will eventually become your thesis title with change and modification. This is how you arrive to research topic step by step. Now the question is how do we arrive at research topic? What are the criteria of selection of research topic? There are primarily two criteria by which we select research topic:

The first criterion is, *Internal criterion,* which may arise from researcher's own interest, resources, finance and time. Personal interest and values may play an important role in the selection of a topic. Researcher may have different interests but will choose one topic among these interests. However, personal interest is not enough. Because it may lead to value judgement and can become too subjective. This kind of research particularly takes place in academic fields, where a researcher is pursuing higher education.

The second criterion is, *External criterion*, which depends on urgency and importance of community, society, association, convention, synod etc. Here the feasibility of the research and facilities are counted. It is not driven by personal interest but by agency, group, institutions, association or synod etc. In this type of research, the interest of the community, association and synod whether in academy or other area is taken care of. This type of research will ask question like, "How will this research help solve a recognized problem in the functioning of association, convention, synod, institution or a society?" For example, a sponsored researcher may take up problem suggested by an association, convention or synod. This type of question will help the researcher to enlarge the research areas of interest and research possibilities.

2. Factors that Affect the Selection of a Research Topic

There are certain factors that affect the selection of research topic. The following factors may affect the selection of research topic:

2.1. State of Scientific Discipline

The present state of scientific discipline affects the selection of research topic in scientific research. For example, an on-going research project in a particular field will determine the selection of topic, because the areas of research interest in each science keeps on increasing and changing. As the knowledge of the discipline develops, there will be gaps that need to be addressed. This factor will try to fill the gaps through research.

2.2. Social Problem

Societies are beset with a myriad of problems. Many a time these problems propel a researcher to undertake research on a particular social issue. In fact, this is one of the most common sources in doing social research. There are many social issues that draw attention to Indian sociologists and researchers, such as – inequality, negative effects of modernization, impact of social media, communalism, politicization of religion etc. The social issues that the churches face also can be factor in doing research. In fact, in the research project of theological education, research topics will be centered on the issues of society, theology, education, social media etc.

2.3. Personal Values of the Researcher

Personal values of the people are also another factor of selection of research problem. People uphold certain values and principles in their life. They have interest and commitment to those values. These interests and commitments will motivate researchers to undertake research on a particular value of the society. In Christianity we have certain inevitable values that have to be reflected in our individual, community and church life. For example, the values of justice, peace and integration of creation. One may undertake a research on values related to integration of creation, particularly driven by ecological concern.

2.4. Social Premiums

Social premium means that selection of certain research problem may depend on the societal needs, where church, association, synod and convention are also included. The needs of these organization may prompt and propel the researcher to select research problem as per the needs of the organizations. Sometime government, institution, and different agencies provide funding to carry out research. This happens also in universities. In the West some universities set aside fund for on-going research and appoint scholars for that purpose. This is one of the factors that propel to undertake research. This kind of research is sponsored and financed by government, institution and different agencies.

2.5. Practical Consideration

Human society is beset with issues and problems and seek for practical solution/answer to those issues and problems. And sometime a researcher even may undertake research project purely on practical consideration of money and scholarship made available to the researchers. However, that does not suggest the researcher has no commitment whatsoever. But this incentive could be a factor in undertaking a research project.

3. Formulation of Research Topic

Selection of research topic does not happen easily and automatically. Formulation of topic must be specific that is affordable to carry out in scientific way. In the process of formulation, the researcher must be able to recognize the difficulties, be it theoretical or practical. It is the difficulty or problem that will guide our search for answers and solution to that particular problem. The difficulty may be experienced with some social problem, or with the failure of theoretical system or prediction. Identification and formulation of problem and then to formulate a specific topic is more difficult than its solution.

3.1. Originating the Question

In the formulation of research problem originating research questions is very important. As it was pointed out that in any research, particularly in social science, research question is very important. But the question is how to start with? The originating question is the first specific problem which a researcher wants to solve. From where to start and how to start the research question is one of the most difficult tasks in any research project. If the researcher is unable to ask right question, then there cannot be right answer or solution. In theological research, the research questions must align with the research title, statement of the problem, elaboration of the problem and hypotheses.

3.2. Rational of Question

Just asking question is not enough. It must have solid ground and rational behind it. It is necessary to know the reasons behind the question. The researcher needs to ask questions like – Why is the question being raised? If question is answered, will it be beneficial to society? The rational of question helps us to distinguish between a valuable and trivial question. It is also necessary to know whether the question is theoretically or practically sound. The question must have either theoretical or practical utility. It must not neglect either of these two.

3.3. Specifying Question

As a researcher starts working on a research project, a number of questions will come to his/her mind. But he/she must be able to filter them out and specify to a few particular questions and state them clearly. A broad question may be break into several specific questions, so that each question can be answered separately and convincingly by the researcher. It should be clearly stated, how a particular question will be dealt with a particular variable or data. For every question the researcher must have variables or data. The question should be simple, pointed, specific, clear and empirically verifiable. When answers are found to these specific questions, it is possible to find out solution to the problem. In order to do that the researcher must be able to make the problem specific, concrete and objective. The formulation of the topic is the real beginning in a scientific investigation.

4. Conditions and Methods of Problem/Topic Formulation

There are four conditions or methods by which we can formulate our research problem/topic. First, the researcher has to immerse himself/herself systematically in the subject matter through the first-hand observation. It is necessary to do extensive study on literatures related to the subject matter, discuss with experienced people (guide, supervisory committee members) and think and reflect deeply.

Second, the researcher must be well acquainted with the relevant theories and empirical generalization of the research area. He/she should be familiar with the results of the findings in the similar area. In this case extensive literature survey will help the researcher. Already established findings will be handy for the researcher in formulating research topic in the similar area.

Third, the researcher may undertake experiment and discuss the subject matter with learned minds (guides and supervisory committee members). He/she may seek comment on the proposed topic and its formulated problem from the existing authorities. He/she should have open, flexible, critical and curious mind. In the SATHRI system of theological research, there is what is called "Supervisory Committee," comprising of three supervisors, who assess, evaluate and provide suggestions at the assessment period and "Research Committee" that assesses the thesis proposal.

Fourth, the topic must be tangible, manageable and achievable in magnitude. If it is not tangible, manageable and achievable, the researcher will land in problem, wasting time, energy and money. It should not be vague, unclear and unachievable. It should not be opaque with abstract jargons. The research topic should be simple, precise, concise and reader friendly.

Over and above the researcher should be able to suggest some solutions or explanation by himself/herself. He/she must be able to properly define certain concepts in a particular manner so that definitions become workable. There will be times where the researcher will be required to reformulate the research topic. Formulation and reformulation of the topic is an on-going process and, in a sense, no process is final and lasting but at some point, of time there has to be full stop. In any research there is no so called "perfect" proposal.

5. Steps in Formulation of Research Problem/Topic

There are generally four steps in formulating research topic or problem. The first step is to specify the research objectives. There should be a clear statement of objective(s). There should be clear, precise and concise statement of the problem with maximum two or three sentences. Second, the researcher should review the context of the research problem. One should have a clear understanding of the context, whether or not the variables are testable in the given environment. Even if you have right question, the situation or context many not be feasible in that particular time and space. In theological research, particularly in Christian ministry research project, a proper context is inevitable. Without proper context research cannot be done. Research questions must be related to the context or vice versa. Third step is to explore the nature of the research problem. Research problem may range from simple to complex and everything depends on a range of variables and their relationship. The understanding of the nature of research problem/topic enables the researcher to develop effective solutions. In theological research the nature of the problem can be theological, pedagogical, hermeneutical, homiletical, social etc. Then the fourth step is to determine the relationship of variables. This can be done by identifying the variables that affect possible solution to the problem. It helps in deciding to what extend the researcher has control on the process of study. It enables to determine the functional relationship between variables. As mentioned earlier there are mainly independent variables and dependent variables. Despite following all these steps, the researcher must be able to keep his/her mind open for alternative course of action or detour before it gets too late.

Summary

Selection and formulation of research problem is very important in research project. There are factors that influence the selection of research problem, such as – state of scientific discipline, social problem, personal value, social premium and practical consideration. The process of formulation of research problem includes – originating research question, rationalization of questions, and specifying of questions. The researcher needs to follow certain steps in the formulation of research problem, they are – specifying the research objectives, reviewing the context of research problem, exploring the research problem and steps to determine the relationship between variables.

References

Ahuja, Ram. *Research Methods.* Jaipur: Rawat Publications, 2011.

Bhandarkar, P. L. and T. S. Williams. *Methodology and Technique of Social Research.* Hyderabad: Himalaya Publishing House, 1994.

Dwivedi, R. S. *Research Methods in Behavioural Sciences.* Delhi: MacMillan India Limited, 1997.

Ghose, B. N. *Scientific Method and Social Research.* New Delhi: Sterling Publishers Private Limited, 2011.

Chapter 7

Concept, Theory, Hypothesis and Variable

Introduction

This chapter delves on the concept, theory, hypothesis and variable of research. These components are very important and vital in any research project. Without proper conceptual or theoretical framework, the researcher will not be able to develop any theory or model for any research concern. To develop a workable model or theory, a workable hypothesis is inevitable. To build up a workable theory or model, a researcher needs to work out different variables.

1. Concept

The term concept denotes an idea that is expressed in words. A concept is an abstraction of an observed thing, phenomenon or events. McClelland, cited by Bhandarkar and Wilkinson, defines the term, as "a short-hand representation of a variety of facts. Its purpose is to simply thinking by subsuming a number of events under one general heading." It consists of both words and definition that a researcher tries to express and articulate in a given research process. By concept a researcher tries to name possible or imagined properties of things or events. Sometime concept of a research problem may be obvious, tangible and achievable but sometime they may not be obvious. When it is not obvious then the researcher may have to spend considerable time and energy to make it obvious and clear. For example, tall, poverty, fast and fearless of a person are obvious but concepts like empathy and love may not be obvious. Concepts are needed to formulate and give expression in words of a research problem and to design as to how to solve it. Concepts are implicit and that implicit concepts are needed to be explicated through clear-cut definition by words. Explication of concept can be done in two ways – 1) by defining in abstract terms, giving general meaning they are intended to convey, which is called 'formal definition' and 2) by defining concepts in terms of the operation, known as 'operational definition' or 'working definition.' Ultimately, concepts have to be expressed through definition(s). Getting good workable definition for a research problem is not that easy. There are certain ways by which we can refine definition of a research problem. First, by examining many definitions of the concept, past and present. Second, trying to get core meaning in which most of the definitions seem to point. Third, based on the core definition, formulate tentative definition. Fourth, looking at the tentative definition, whether or not it covers all cases undertaken for study and related in reaching the objectives. Fifth, by submitting the definition for critical appraisal comprising both scientists (theologians) and non-scientists (non-theologians) and finally, making revision based on legitimate criticism received.

2. Conceptualization

We can refer to the theoretical system of the science as a *conceptual system.* Each science develops its own terms, or *concepts,* for communicating its findings. We use these terms to stand for the phenomena or aspects of phenomena we are investigating. Consequently, when we formulate a proposition, we use concepts as *symbols* of the phenomena we are studying. Since we directly deal with only *concept,* we quite often confuse the *concept* with the *phenomenon,* it is supposed to symbolize.

Since all these concepts are abstractions and represent only certain aspects of reality, it becomes important to know (1) which aspects we should study, and (2) how to develop concepts for them. The first problem properly belongs in a discussion of theories and hypothesis.

Then we need to do the process of conceptualization and can be treated in the following ways (a) the concept as abstraction, (b) concepts and communication, (c) problem of definition, (d) reconceptualization, and (e) the operational definition. The process of conceptualization is one of abstracting and generalizing sense expression. Concept and conceptualization are not only needed for science but *they are the foundation of human communication and thought.*

2.1. Concept as Abstraction

Concepts are logical construct created from sense perception, precepts or even fairly complex experiences. The assumption that concepts actually exist in phenomena leads to many errors. The concept is not the phenomenon itself. Logical constructs do not exist outside the stated frame of reference. The failure to recognize this is termed the *fallacy of reification,* which is, *treating abstraction as if they were actual phenomena.* An example of reification is, W. I. Thomas' *Four Wishes* (1) experiencing new situation (2) securing the recognition of other (3) retaining feelings of security and (4) eliciting response from other, were reified by readers, while they labelled for conceptual convenience. These *Four Wishes* of W.

I. Thomas were reified by readers about the causes of happy life. But there can be other causes for a happy life apart from these causes.

Both facts and concepts are abstraction. A concept like a fact is an abstraction, not a phenomenon. The distinction between fact and concept is that concepts symbolize the empirical relationship and phenomena, which are stated by the fact. A fact is logical construct of concepts. A concept in turn, is abstracted from many expressions or precepts.

Concepts, however, are obviously not only basic to scientific method alone: *they are the foundation of all human communication and thought.* However, science requires greater precision in communication, the process of conceptualization must be more conscious and rigorous.

2.2. Concepts and Communication

Concepts in science must be communicable in a very special sense. They must not arouse just vague "feeling," but must be so constructed that all their components are known. Deriving and clarifying the elements of construct are the major processes of definition, basic to the general problem of generalization. Due to differences between the common-sense of the public and the scientific way of looking at the world as discussed earlier, careful definition has a paradoxical quality. On one hand it facilitates communication within the science but on the other it raises barriers to the lay understanding of scientific concepts. The common complaint is that science uses big words. The problem is also prevalent among the scientists themselves. Because of different vocabularies among different disciplines the gap of communication seems to be wide.

The gap between social science and physical science is wide. For example, in biology terms such as: "specific adsorption," "antibody molecules," "angstrom units," "antigenic protein," "diluted antiserum," and "heterologous serum," are difficult to understand even to the well-educated people.

2.3. Problems in Definition and Communication

Concepts are developed from a shared experience. For example, why the German word *gemutlic* is difficult to translate in English? Why the German words *Gemeinschaft* and *Gesellschaft* are still used in the original German form? Why the word *Gymnasium* been taken from German but given different referent in English? *Gemutlic* refers to a warm, pleasant, relaxed, and "feeling-at-homeness." *Gemeinshaft* and *Gesellshaft* refer to "community" and "society" in English. Why the German *Festschrift* (*Fest* means "celebration" or "feast and *Schrift* means "writing) is still used which means "celebration writing" or "celebration publication" or "celebratory (piece of) writing? Because, this concept is difficult to translate in one word in English.

The term used to denote scientific concepts may also have meanings in other frame of reference. Frequently the terms are constructed from Greek or Latin roots, generally, from the first person who first elaborated the concept. For the students in physics "mass" does not mean a "big pile of something." In anthropology and sociology, the term "culture" does not refer to an acquaintanceship with opera, painting, literature or "good" manner, but rather to the totality of the social heritage of any society. In sociology the term "bureaucracy" can mean many things, such as, red tapes, administrative waste, and official disregard for public interest etc. A term may refer to different phenomena, for example, *function*. The term *function* can mean different things depending on the discipline one undertakes. Different terms may refer to the same phenomenon: For example, "structure-function," "ideal-real," "formal-informal," and "primary-secondary." A term may have no immediate empirical referent at all.

The meaning of concepts may change in time and space. For example, "social structure" may mean many things. In social science it means continuous *patterned* activity and that is the central characteristics of social structure. Such concept, then, has very complex referents, through other concepts, before the empirical reference is clear. Ultimately, there will be empirical referent, but the basic concept refers to logical relationship between other concepts. But it must be admitted that the *ultimate* empirical referents of a concept be determinable. Those, who use such concepts, are unaware of the fact that they have no empirical referent.

The meaning of concept may change with the change of *focus*. Attention may be centered upon different *aspects* of the same concept in such a way so as to change its meaning, although the same term is kept. "Intelligence" is another example. Earlier it was understood by psychologists as being inherited, fairly stable intellectual potential. But because of the growth and application of "Artificial Intelligence," the understanding of intelligence has changed drastically.

2.4. Reconceptualization

In the course of doing research, need may arise for "Reconceptualization" and "Respecification" of a concept. A careful student will compare some of these hints with later discussions of the hypothesis, the logic of proof, the formulation of questions, and the analysis of data. How is it done? Reconceptualization is done as follows:

2.4.1. After writing out the preliminary statement of the project, the student should carefully select from the statement a list of major concepts.

2.4.2. An analysis of the apparent *meaning elements* should be made.

2.4.3. It would then be useful to refer to the published literatures in which the concept has been used, in order to discover the various uses of the term.

2.4.4. By relating the phenomenon with other phenomenon, which has been described by *other terms*, and often other fields.

Respecification of the concept always leads to more fruitful *hypotheses*. Respecification means making the concepts more specific. If the concepts are not specific enough then finding answers to particular research problem will not be focussed enough.

3. Construct

The terms 'concept' and 'construct' have similar meaning but there is difference between the two. While concepts are mental construct and abstract, construct is observable and measurable. A construct is a concept devised to aid in scientific analysis and generalization. A construct is observable derived from concept. For example, 'intelligence' is concept but intelligence quotient (IQ) is construct. We reduce intelligence into IQ through the device, IQ=MA/CA x100 (Mental Age divided by Chronological age x 100 = IQ). If IQ of a person is 130, it is observable and measurable and that is the construct (IQ) of concept (Intelligence).

4. Theory and Fact

Patton defines, "Theory denotes to a set of well-developed categories (e.g. themes, concepts) that are systematically interlaced through statements and relationship to form a theoretical framework that explains some relevant, psychological, educational, nursing or other phenomenon. The statements of *relationship* explain who, what, when, where, why and how and consequences, or events occur." Strauss and Corbin define theory as "... A theory is usually more than a set of findings, it offers an explanation about phenomenon."

There is popular misconception that science is thought to be concerned only with facts and not with theory. It is generally thought the theory (speculation) is the domain of philosophers. However, in regards to the relationship between theory and fact, we must remember that (1) theory and fact are not diametrically opposed to each other, but inextricably intertwined; (2) theory is not speculation and (3) scientists are very much concerned with both theory and fact.

A fact is regarded as an *empirically verifiable observation. Theory refers to the relationships between facts,* or to the ordering of them in some meaningful way.

Theory is a tool of science: (1) it defines the major orientation of a science, by defining the kinds of data which are to be abstracted; (2) it offers a conceptual scheme by which the relevant phenomena are systematized, classified, and interrelated; (3) it summarizes facts into (a) empirical generalization and (b) systems of generalization (4) it predicts facts; and (5) it points to gaps in our knowledge.

Facts are also productive of theory- (a) facts help to initiate theories; (2) they lead to reformulation of existing theory; (3) they cause the rejection of theories which do not fit the facts; (4) they change the focus and orientation of theory; and (5) they clarify and redefine theory.

4.1. The Role of Theory

Theory helps reorient any research problem. Theory has role in conceptualization and classification. A theory summarizes (1) empirical generalizations, and (2) system of relationships between propositions. Theory predicts facts. Theory points to gaps in our knowledge

4.2. The Role of Fact

Fact initiates theory. Facts lead to the rejection and reformulation of existing theory. Facts redefine and clarify theory.

5. Hypothesis/Hypotheses

Aa stated earlier, hypothesis is a well stated and framed statement for what we are looking for to investigate. When facts are assembled, ordered, and seen in the relationships, they constitute a theory. A theory is not a speculation, but built upon on facts. Now, various facts in a theory may be analysed, and relationships other than those stated in the theory can be deduced. At this point there is no knowledge as to whether such deductions are correct or incorrect. The formulation of the deduction, however, constitutes a hypothesis. If verified, it becomes part of a future theoretical construction. One scientist, in the relationship between theory and hypothesis comments: "In practice a theory is an elaborate hypothesis which deals with more types of facts than and does simple hypothesis. …The distinction … is not clearly defined." Although, these two can never be satisfactorily separated, it is useful to think them as two aspects of the way in which science adds to knowledge.

Theory states a logical relationship between facts. From theory other propositions can be deduced and that *should* be true. *These deduced propositions are hypotheses.* A hypothesis looks forward. It is a proposition which can be put to test to determine its validity. It may prove to be correct or incorrect. In any event, however, *it leads to an empirical test.* Whatever the outcome may be, the hypothesis is a question put in such a way that an answer of some kind can be forthcoming.

Every worth-while theory, then, permits formulation of additional hypotheses. These, when tested, can either be proved or disproved, and in turn constitute further list of the original theory. Formulation in useful hypothesis is one of the most difficult steps in scientific method.

5.1. Problems in Formulating Hypothesis

Formulating a hypothesis is not an easy task. However, how difficult, it might be in formulating a hypothesis, without it, research is unfocussed, a random empirical wandering. Hypothesis is a must in scientific research. Hypothesis is the necessary link between theory and investigation which leads to the discovery of additions to knowledge. Three difficult roads in formulating hypothesis are as follows:

a. Absence of (or the absence of knowledge of) a clear theoretical framework.
b. Lack of ability to utilize that theoretical framework logically.
c. Failure to be acquainted with available research techniques, so as to be able to phrase the hypothesis properly.

Framing logical and testable question is also not an easy task as just how difficult is it to ask an important, testable question. In the same way it is difficult to formulate a testable hypothesis. Therefore, we need to start with a "working hypothesis."

5.2. Types of Hypotheses

There are three broad levels of hypotheses:

a. Some hypotheses state the existence of empirical uniformities.
b. Some hypotheses are concerned with complex ideal types.
c. Some hypotheses are concerned with relation of analytic variables.

Further, it also can be grouped in two types, namely null hypothesis (Ho) and alternative hypothesis (H_1). The simple understanding of null hypothesis and alternative hypothesis is that while null hypothesis proposes an issue negatively, alternative hypothesis proposes positive proposition for the solution of an issue/problem. For example, if null hypothesis proposes "social media does not have impact on the spiritual life of youths" the alternative hypothesis would propose "social media has impact on the spiritual life of youths." As null hypothesis is implied in any research project, there is no need of explicit mention of null hypothesis, especially in qualitative research.

Hypothesis is a necessary condition for successful research. The formulation of hypothesis must be given considerable attention, to clarify its relation to theory, remove vague or terms with value judgment, and specify the test to be applied. Hypothesis may be formulated on different levels of abstraction

5.3. How to Generate Hypothesis

In science, we do not take things for granted. What we know by common sense is not scientifically known fact. That's why, scientific world would say, "What everybody known is not known until it has been tested." Hypothesis/Hypotheses may be generated as follows:

a. Some hypotheses are concerned with the relation of analytic variables.
b. The general culture, in which a science develops, furnishes many of its basic hypotheses. For example, in the Western culture, a hypothesis with the question of happiness and "how to be happy" may necessarily come from the Western culture itself. However, in the East the understanding of happiness may differ from the West.

c. Hypotheses originate the science itself. For example, from "opinion leader," one may find that it is in the category of "the influential person"- cosmopolitan to local.
d. Analogies are often a source of useful hypothesis. Causal observation in nature or in the framework of another science could be source of hypothesis.
e. Hypotheses are also consequence of personal, idiosyncratic experience.

5.4. Characteristics of Hypotheses: Some Criteria for Judging Hypotheses

a. The hypotheses must be conceptually clear: What to do: Write a list of concepts
b. The hypotheses should have empirical referents. What to do: First, analyse the concepts which express attitude rather than describing or referring to empirical phenomenon.
c. The hypotheses must be specific. What to do: Never be satisfied with a general prediction, if it can be broken to more precise hypotheses.
d. Hypotheses should be related to available techniques. What to do: Look for research articles on the subject being investigated by many techniques. Make a list of various techniques.
e. The hypotheses should be related to a body of theory. What to do: First, cover the literature relating to your subject. Second, try to abstract from literature the way in which various proposition and sets of propositions relate to one another. Third, ascertain whether you can deduce any of the propositions, including your own hypothesis.

6. Variable

In social science research, instead of "cause" and "effect" technical terms independent variable and dependent variable are used. In experiment research the terms treatment variable and outcome variable are also used. Treatment variable is also called experimental variable. But independent variable and dependent variable are the mostly used terms in experimental and non-experimental research. Along with independent variable and dependent variable we have what is called "control" variable in between independent variable and dependent variable. Control variable(s) signifies a variable whose effect the researcher wants to use.

Variable is characteristic that of two or more values. It is a characteristic that is common to a number of individuals, groups, events, objects etc. It is that varies. For example, for age group – young, middle age, old age groups, for income – lower class, middle class, upper class etc.

There is a close connection between variable and category, which may create confusion to the common people. For example, gender is a variable, consisting of two categories – male and female. Community is also variable with two categories – urban and rural.

The analysed variables are called *explanatory* variable and all others are called *extraneous* variable. *Extraneous* variables are categorized as *controlled* and *uncontrolled* variables. Controlled or control variables control the limits and the focus of the study. For example, if the study is on youth, the age group will cover 15-24 years and all other age groups are excluded. This will reflect in inclusion and exclusion criteria. The various types of variables are described as follows:

6.1. Independent Variables (IV) and Dependent Variables (DV)

In any social science/empirical research, there will be independent and dependent variables. Independent variable is the assumed cause of dependent variables. In statistic independent variable is called X variable and dependent variable is called Y variable. Simply put, independent variable is a cause and dependent variable is an effect. For example, A causes B, here A is independent variable and B is dependent variable. In any research problem there will be causes and effects of any issue or problem. Let us take the example of a teacher, who wants to know which method of teaching is more effective in teaching for children, such as – lecture method, visual method or game method or combination of two or more methods. Here the teaching method is independent variable and the effects on children is dependent variable. We need to keep in mind that sometime dependent variable also can be independent variable. For example, farmers' income and quality of life. Here income is independent variable and quality of life is dependent variable. We must keep in mind that sometime independent variable also can become dependent variable. For example, let us make a hypothesis "higher the income, better the quality of life." Here income is independent variable and quality of life dependent variable. But income could become dependent variable because income/produce may depend on availability of water supply. Therefore, availability of water becomes independent variable and income/produce become dependent variable.

There is what is called *intervening* variable between independent variable and dependent variable. For example, take the example of a hypothesis of a cultivator and land holding. Our hypothesis is, lower the land holding, higher the poverty or vice versa. But despite having high land holding a cultivator may land up in poverty, because land is not properly utilized or due to lack of good seed or lack of manure or lack of proper irrigation and so on. Here, seed, manure, irrigation might intervene farmer's production and his/her income and can cause poverty.

a. Some Examples of IV and DV

Hypothesis 1: Under social reinforcement conditions middle class children will learn significantly more than working class children.

IV: Middle class versus working class.

DV: Amount learned.

Hypothesis 2: BD theological students who plan to pursue higher studies are more serious and hardworking than other students.

IV: BD students who plan to pursue higher studies.

DV: Serious, hardworking

Hypothesis 3: Theological students with positive academic self-concept will gain significantly higher grade than students with negative self-concept.

IV: Theological students with positive academic self-concept and students with negative academic self-concept.

DV: Grade

6.2. Experimental and Measured Variables

Experimental variables describe the details of the researcher's treating of a problem of research and measured variables refer to the measurement of the data done in the process of research. For example, if we examine the effectiveness of theological education, we examine the availability of books, library, infrastructure, well qualified teachers etc. There are four levels of measurement – nominal level, ordinal level, interval level and ratio.

6.3. Measurement of Variables

a. Nominal level: Nominal means name. Nominal scale does not measure but names. Nominal level is the easiest type of measurement. It is unidirectional and exclusive classification of categorization of categories of events or phenomena. For example, male-female, Hindu-Christian, rural-urban etc. It is a simple classification of different categories of phenomena.
b. Ordinal Level: Ordinal measurement put data in the rank order. It does not only include categorization but also ranking. It is ranking of continuum of high-low. For example, first rank, second rank, third rank or in economic term lower class, middle class, upper class. In exam, poor, good, excellent, outstanding and extra ordinary. In terms of social cohesion in India, say *favourable, very favourable, neutral, unfavourable* or *very unfavourable.*
c. Interval Level: It gives information about the distance between values and contain equal intervals, for example 5th, 10th and 15th grade students. In each of these variables, interval is 5. Or in IQ level of three students are 100, 110, and 125. In this it means that IQ level of second student is 10 points higher than the first student and the third student is 15 points higher than the second student.
d. Ratio Level: In ratio, to make statement one needs a true zero point. It is proportion and ratio. It relates to one value to the other. For example, a) a person's weight is 40 kilos and the other is 80 kilos. This means that the second person is twice heavier than the first person. b) the difference between 10 degrees

Centigrade and 20 degrees Centigrade is equal to that between of 30 and 40 degrees Centigrade. Or 20 Centigrade is twice as high a temperature as 10 degrees Centigrade.

6.4. Univariate, Bivariate and Multivariate

There are mainly three types of analysis of variable, such as -Univariate, Bivariate and Multivariate. These three variates are the commonly used in data analysis, particularly in quantitative research.

a. Univariate

Univariate analysis is a technique for examining data for one variable at a time. The goal of univariate analysis is to get clear picture of the data by examining one variable of a given research one at a time. This is done as a part of the prelude to more complex analysis or as a part of basic descriptive study. The data are analysed in various forms, such as – tables, charts, graphs and statistical indexes. The nature of technique depends on whether researcher is analysing variables measuring at the nominal/ordinal or interval/ ratio levels. In any research, if there is less variables, then it becomes difficult to detect how differences in one variable is related to differences in another variable. The difficulty arises when there is more than one variable.

Any variable organized in a table is called frequency distribution. A frequency distributing is first created listing the responses in categories and adding up the number of cases that occur in each category. Let us take a question, for example for BD students, frequency of distribution of fear of failing in language exam (either Greek and Hebrew), such as *do you fear in failing language exam?* with the responses/ categories of "yes," "no," "don't know," and "no response." After conducting investigation in the three theological colleges affiliated to Senate of Serampore with 50 BD students each (total 150), the finding is found say, "yes" is 70, "no" is 50, "don't know" is 20 and "no response" is 10, these mere frequency number will not say anything. We need to provide a standard or reference point by which we can interpret the data. Here the Percentage Distribution comes into play. The percentage distribution can provide an explicit comparative framework for interpreting distribution. To create percentage distribution, you divide the number of cases in each category by total number of cases and multiply by 100. For example:

Sl. No.	Label	Frequency	Percentage
1.	Yes	70	47%
2.	No	50	33%
3.	Don't know	20	13%
4.	No Response	10	7%
	Total	150	100%

b. Bivariate Analysis

Bivariate analysis is the examination of the relationship between two variables. The objective of bivariate analysis is to assess the variables. It involves two variables. For example, fear of failing in language exam and spending time in social media. It is to determine whether relationship exist between the two variables. It will determine whether spending more time in social media is the cause of fear of failing in language exam. Here the spending more time is cause and the failing in language exam is effect. It will also analyse how much effect or influence one variable has on the other. Alike, univariate analysis, the way in which this is done depends on the level of measurement.

c. Multivariate Analysis

As stated in above section we have bivariate that calculate the association or correlation between two variables. Bivariate provides basis for predicting the values of variable from another values. However, to test causal and complex hypothesis bivariate association is never sufficient. Therefore, multivariate analysis is necessary to interpret data. Multivariate analysis is the analysis of multiple variables in a given research. For example, use social of media may not be the cause of fear of failing in language exam. There could be other variable for the fear of failing in language. There could be another cause for such effect.

Summary

The chapter seven discussed concept, theory, hypothesis and variable, which are essential parts of a research project. The term concept is an idea which is expressed in words. A researcher can have many concepts or ideas, but those ideas need to be expressed in words. The process of expression of concept is called conceptualization. To make concepts clear and succinct reconceptualization may be required. After conceptualization of certain ideas, theory can be built based on facts. While, fact is regarded as a verifiable observation, theory refers to the relationship between facts. Theory is a tool of science. A hypothesis is a well stated and framed statement for what we are looking to investigate. Variable is characteristic of two or more values. There are different types of variables – Independent Variable (IV), Dependent Variable DV), Intervening Variable (IV), Experimental variable and Measured variable. There are various kinds of analysis of variables, such as – univariate, bivariate and multivariate. Univariate is the technique for examining data for one variable at a time. Bivariate analysis is the examination of the relationship between two variables. Multivariate analysis is the analysis of multiple variables in a given research.

References

Ahuja, Ram, *Research Method,* Reprint Jaipur: Rawat Publications, 2011.

Bhandarkar, P. L. and T. S. Wilkinson. *Methodology and Technique of Social Research.* Ninth Edition. Bombay, Delhi, Nagpur: Himalaya Publishing House, 1992.

Goode, William J. and Paul K. Hutt. *Methods in Social Research,* First Indian Reprint. Delhi: Surjeet Publication, 2006.

Patton, Michael Quinn. *Qualitative Method & Evaluation Method,* 3rd edition. Thousand Oaks; London; New Delhi: SAGE Publications, 2002.

Punch, Keith F. *Introduction to Social Research: Quantitative and Qualitative Approaches,* Second Edition. Los Angeles; London; New Delhi; Singapore: SAGE Publications, 2005.

Chapter 8

Data Collection Methods-1

Introduction

Data collection is one of the most important steps in research project. The task of data collection begins after research problem has been defined, topic chosen and design worked out. Without the collection of data, analysis and interpretation, there cannot be research. Particularly, in social science research, data collection is inevitable. In data collection, a researcher may use various methods. The primary goal of data collection is to ensure quality data or evidence that will help to reach to conclusion or find answer to a particular problem. Data collection is concerned with accurate acquisition of data. It is essential to ensure integrity of research. It is the process of gathering and measuring data. In the following chapters we will see some methods by which researchers can collect data.

1. Types of Data Collection Method

There are mainly two types of data collection, primary data collection and secondary data collection. The primary data collection is a form of collecting data afresh or for the first time. Thus, it is original in character. Primary data collection is done in survey and descriptive research. In descriptive research, primary data is obtained through observation or direct communication with respondents in one form or another or personal interview. Secondary data collection, on the other hand, is collected data already by someone else and already passed through statistical process. These types of data are already available, analysed and used in published or unpublished work. In the use of secondary data, the researcher must be very careful, because the data available may be unsuitable. In this chapter we will see two types of data collection methods – observation method and questionnaire method.

2. Methods of Data Collection

2.1. Observation Method

It is said that science starts with observation and ends with observation. Observation is not casual looking at certain phenomenon but planned and methodical watching that involves constraints to improve accuracy. It is selection, provocation, recording and encoding certain information from certain behaviour or phenomenon. Selection means that there is focus in observation. Provocation means that though the observers do not destroy natural settings, they can make subtle changes in natural setting for clarity. Recording means that the observer records events/incidents for analysis. Encoding means simplification of records or deciphering them. As mentioned earlier this method is popularly used in the collection of primary data. It applies eyes rather than ears and voice. Observation is not casual but intentional, deliberate, accurate watching and noting a particular phenomenon as it occurs with regard to the cause and effect or of mutual relations.

There are two types of observation methods – participants and non-participants which we have discussed in the first chapter but they are discussed in more detail as follows:

2.2. Participant Observation

In participant observation research method in certain cases, the researcher may have to disguise himself/herself as to be accepted as a member of the group. In this method the researcher carries out investigation exactly participating in the activities as others do in the group. The researcher may find role in the group which will not disturb the usual patterns of the group. A sociologist may enter the community as a local historian or a botanist. An anthropologist also may follow the same principle. It can be taken for granted that if the members are *unaware* of the researcher's purpose, their behaviour is least likely to be affected. In this method, one can record the "natural" behaviour of the group. To the extent that the researcher actually participates, many of his/her emotional reaction will be similar to that of true members. Researcher will have access to the body of knowledge that others will not have. He/she will have greater depth of experience by being able to record the actual activities of other participants. In this method, the range of material collection will be much wider. He/she will be able to record the context which gives meaning to expression of opinion.

2.3. Problems in Participant Observation

In participatory observation research method, the problem is that the researcher might narrow down his/her range of experience, paradoxically. He/she may take side on a particular position of the group, with a definite clique or friendship circle. He/she would learn a pattern of activity which is characteristic of its members, and thus less able to find out what fringe individuals are doing. If there is hierarchy of power, or a stratification of prestige, he/she may come to occupy within it, then many avenues of information will be closed. Then group behaviour will change, to the extent he/she participates emotionally, then he/she loses objectivity. He/she may react in anger and can become emotional. He/she might seek prestige or ego satisfaction. He/she might sympathize with tragedy, may not record it upon his/her fellow members. As the researcher learns the "correct" modes of behaviour, he/she may come to take for granted that they seem to be perfectly natural. As a result, he/she might frequently fail to note details.

Citing Festinger and Katz (1976), Ahuja (2011) outlines six fundamental problems in participant observation as follows:

a. Under what condition observation to be made? How is observation situation be structured?
b. What behaviour should be selected or recorded in order to obtain required information.
c. How stable are the conditions on which observation can be made, so that same results may be obtained? Are they reliable?
d. What is the validity of the process which has been observed or inferred?
e. What evidence is there that some process with functional unity is being observed?
f. Has attempt been able to summarize what is observed in quantitative terms? Can a score be assigned?

2.4. Non-participant Observation

Non-participant observation method may provide some remedies to the problems faced in participant observation method. A researcher may participate in fishing trip but during preparation for an important religious event he/she will interview formally the important events or record the ritual chants during the ceremony. However, purely nonparticipant observation is difficult. Also, it is almost impossible for the outsider to be a genuine participant in all ways. Therefore, both participant and nonparticipant observation methods have to be used which is a classic pattern in social research. Consequently, nonparticipant observation method is, then, usually "quasi-participant" observation. The researcher also needs to be a good listener. In any rate in a research work, whether participant or non-participant the identification of the research problem is the most important task. Now the question is, how to go about with it? The followings are some steps that we can take up.

a. We can have field experience log, in a form of diary, or it may be a daily record, where we can note down each item.
b. In that experience log or daily record, we can have subheadings, say, with "socialization" for better categorization and organization of the findings.
c. Having running notes will be beneficial for the researcher.
d. Then the researcher can make a complete record.
e. Whether or not the original notes are recorded in subheadings, they must be analysed and placed under the appropriate categories.
f. Analysis of notes show, however, that emphasis has been placed upon other types of data.
g. It helps to correct errors while field work is in progress.
h. Although, researcher may have time to carry out systematic coding and indexing operations, but even

preliminary categorization is useful if it is done each day.

i. It is useful to record both observation and interpretation of observation.
j. It is absolutely essential that continuing analysis and reports be made while the field work is underway.
k. It is helpful that colleagues see the research records, which are not in the field.

3. Questionnaire Method

Through this method a researcher can collect lots of information from respondents to a series of questions. Developing questionnaire takes time and effort. The researcher has to develop the questions systematically and sequentially. In this method list of questions are prepared by the researcher relating to research problem and distribute to various respondents. There are, therefore, two types of process in questionnaire method – development of questionnaire and distribution of questionnaire. Distribution can be done in various ways – even through email and WhatsApp. The questionnaire should be drafted in a proper and simple way so that the respondents can understand easily. It is widely used in large research projects as there is chance to get large number of samples of the study. This method is used by government organizations, research institutions, private companies and research scholars. This method is often used in theological research, especially in Christian ministry.

The questionnaire method can be further divided into two categories-*structured* and *non-structured.* Structured questionnaire contains a number of questions with a prescribed sequence. The researcher prepares the questions in order so that respondents will be able to answer without ambiguity and problem. In non-structured, the questionnaire does not have sequence. There is no prescribed sequence in the preparation of questions. The questions can be both *close ended* questions and *open-ended* questions.

3.1. Some Characteristics of Good Questionnaire

a. It deals with a significant topic, which the respondent will recognize as important enough to warrant time and effort.

b. It seeks only the information that cannot be obtained through other sources.

c. It should be attractive in appearance, neatly and beautifully printed.

d. The questions should be objective so that they do not lead to researcher's desire.

e. The questions should be from general to specific.

f. There should not be grammatical and spelling mistakes.

g. There should be clear directions, important terms defined, each question is worded in simple way as clearly as possible.

h. It should not be too long.

Summary

Science begins with observation and ends with observation. Observation is one of the most important methods of data collection in any research project. There are mainly two types of observation – participant observation and non-participant observation. In participant observation method, the researcher carries out investigation by participating in the activities of the group. In non-participant observation method, the researcher does not get involved in the activities of the group but observed as an outsider. Complete non-participant observation is not possible therefore, quasi-participant method is better to get more reliable information. Questionnaire is another method by which a lot information can be collected. Questionnaire can be structured and unstructured. In this method the researcher prepares and distribute questions to various respondents related to the research problem.

References

Ahuja, Ram. *Research Method.* Jaipur: Rawat Publications, 2018.

Babu, G. Ramesh. *Research Methodology in Social Sciences.* New Delhi: Concept Publishing Company, 2008.

Bhandarkar, P. L. and T. S. Wilkinson. *Methodology and Techniques of Social Research.* Bombay: Himalaya Publishing House, 1994.

Goode, William J. and Paul K. Hutt. *Methods in Social Research.* Delhi: Surjeet Publications, 2007.

Kothari, C. R. *Research Methodology: Methods and Techniques.* New Delhi: Viwsa Prakashan, 1995.

Nalwa, Vanit. *The ABC of Research for Behavioural and Social Science.* Madras: Wiley Eastern Limited, 1992.

Saravanavel, P. *Research Methodology.* Allahabad: Kitab Mahal, 2011.

Sharma, P. K. *Research Methodology.* New Delhi: Maxford Books, 2013.

Thakur, Devendra. *Research Methodology in Social Sciences.* Rajouri: DEEP & DEEP Publications. 2008.

Chapter 9

Data Collection Methods-2

Introduction

We continue to discuss on the method of data collection in this chapter. This chapter dwells on the Interview, Focus Group, Documentary, Oral Tradition/History, Artefacts, Written Documents and Audio-Visual-Digital methods. They are important methods for the research in social science. As in theological education, social science is also used across various disciplines, such as – theology, biblical studies, history of Christianity, education, counselling, missiology etc. Having a fare knowledge about these methods is inevitable in theological education research.

1. Interview Method

Interview method is one of the most commonly used methods in social science research. It is a kind of obtaining data through verbal techniques. It is a direct method of data collection. It is a method of collection from primary sources. It is both qualitative and quantitative research depending on the nature of the research. There are primarily three types of interview methods – Structured Interview, Unstructured Interview and Semi-Structured Interview.

2. Types of Interview Method

2.1. Structured Interview

In this type of research, the researcher uses well defined and highly standardized prepared questions during the time of interview. Questions are structured logically and sequentially leading one to the next. Here the interview takes place according to written instructions given in the schedule. In the structured interview method, the respondent is asked series of pre-established questions, with pre- set response categories. All respondents receive same questions with no room for variation. Flexibility and variations are minimized. In this type of method, the interviewer attempts to play neutral role in a neutral manner.

2.2. Unstructured Interview

In this method of research, the interviewer does not follow pre-planned set of questions. The interviewer has freedom to ask any question related to the problem of any research undertaken without any sequence. In this type of method, a deep knowledge and skill is required on the part of the interviewer. There is flexibility and spontaneity. This type of interview allows for unexpected response from the respondent. It is open-ended and in-depth interview. Sometime it is also called ethnographic interview. It does not have *a priori* generalization. Fontana and Frey have outlined seven aspects of unstructured interview as follows:

a. Accessing the setting of the research.
b. Understanding the language and culture of the people.

c. Deciding on how the researcher present himself/ herself.
d. Locating the informants among the population.
e. Gaining trust from the people under study.
f. Establishing rapport with the people.
g. Collecting empirical materials needed for the research.

2.3. Semi-structured Interview

As the name suggests in this type of interview, the interviewer asks only few structured questions, while the rest of the questions are unplanned in advance. The questions do not have fixed wording or order. Questions are not specific. It is a combination of structured and unstructured questions. In the course of interview, the interviewer might take detour of interview. Here the nature of question is generally open-ended in order to gain richer information about attitude and behaviour of the respondents.

2.4. Feminist Perspective on Interview Method

Feminist research makes use of semi-structured and unstructured interview. It also redefines interview in significant ways. Feminist perspective sees traditional interviewing as masculine paradigm, embedded in masculine culture, stressing masculine traits and excluding sensitivity, emotionality and other traits. Traditional interviewing is considered scientific and positivist, requiring objectivity and detachment, but feminist interview stresses openness, emotional engagement and development of trust. Feminist interviewing is non-hierarchical. This perspective considers that traditional interviewing is paternalistic, condescending in its attitude towards women and does not account the gender differences. It alleges that the traditional interviewing portrays hierarchical relationship and subordinate women in societal position.

2.5. Process of Interview

a. The interviewer must give proper introduction to interviewee.
b. After short self-introduction, the interviewer should explain the nature and purpose of research.
c. The interviewer should be able to create an atmosphere where the interviewee can express himself/herself freely.
d. The interviewer must be able to prompt the memory of interviewee in the process of interview.
e. The questions should be put in a systematic way and lucid in language.
f. At the time of interview, the interviewer must jot down important points between brief pauses. With due permission even one can record in audio or video.
g. The interview should not be closed abruptly but give to natural end. There should not be hurry. Before ending the interview, major points should be summarized.
h. After the interview is over, the interviewer must write down the report.
i. One should never forget to appreciate and thank the interviewee.

2.6. Practical Aspects of Interview

In practical aspect of interview, the following concerns need to be taken into account:

a. Who will be interviewed and why?

b. How many people will be interviewed and how many times each person will be interviewed?
c. When and how long each respondent be interviewed?
d. Where each respondent will be interviewed?
e. How will access to the interview situation be organized?

2.7. Managing the Interview

a. Preparation for the interview, interview schedule.
b. Bringing the interviewee and establishing rapport.
c. Communication and listening skills.
d. Asking questions, the sequence and the types of questions.
e. Closing the interview.
f. Recording the interview.

3. Focus Group

The Focus Group method is discussion-based interview. It is qualitative research and generated through group discussion. The roll of the researcher is more of moderator or facilitator. The researcher or moderator will be moderating, facilitating, monitoring and recording group interaction. It is a group of people that interact with one another led by a moderator on common interest or characteristics focussed on a specific issue in order to gain maximum possible information. It is a research technique to collect data through group interaction on a certain topic determined by the researcher. Focus group can be used as self-contained method or this technique may be used in conjunction with other methods. There is flexibility in this method, which is one of the advantages of this method. It helps a researcher to be more open. Focus group, however, is perceived as a quick and easy approach in carrying out research.

Like any other research, focus group also can be done step by step as follows:

3.1. Focus on the Research Purpose

The focus group method should not be just for the sake of focus group. It should not be discussion just for the sake of discussion, not just hearing without listening. It means the researcher must be able to enable participants to listen the discussion attentively in the course of discussion. It should not be short of mere tokenism. It is not explicitly designed to educate the group, resolve conflict or encourage having consensus on certain issue. There should not be any preconceived idea or solution of an issue or problem under discussion on the part of the researcher.

3.2. Selection of a Skilled Moderator

A skilled moderator is needed in this type of research method. The moderator must be able to stimulate discussion. He/she must be confident and comfortable who is able to communicate to the participants precisely. The moderator must be able to create an atmosphere where participants will be at ease in disclosing specific information on a particular issue.

The difference between focus group and the individual interview is that the focus group is on the group, not on individual. Participants directly respond to researcher/moderator and comments made by the group. It is a group activity. The group discussion is affected by social context represented by the group. Participants ask questions that may differ from researcher or moderator. The on-going discussion may give different interpretation in the process. The same individual who offered one view early in the interview may revise his/her view as an outcome of group interaction, comment and expressions. The researcher should never push or expect participants to come to agreement or consensus by any manipulation. Focus group is primary source of data collection and secondary source is based on primary source, it simply copies, interpret or judge found in primary sources.

4. Documentary Method

Documentary sources have to do with the life stories of an individual or a group. It can be an account of the lives of individuals, families or a social group. It also can be on war or on certain events or incidents. It includes diaries, letters, memories, photographs etc. It is related with life stories collected by the researcher, analysed and interpreted. There are two sources in the documentary method – primary source and secondary source. Primary sources are those that are written by the people directly by themselves in a contemporary time or near contemporary time. Primary sources form the basic and original material that provides the researcher raw evidence. In contrary, secondary sources are those that discuss the period studied but not of the same time or otherwise brought somewhat removed from the actual events.

5. Oral Tradition/History

Oral tradition is information of stories, histories, events, myth, and legends passed on orally from generations to generations. These oral traditions are primarily found in illiterate societies. Oral traditions are found in traditional societies. We can use this method when finding documentary sources are slim. It can provide insights about the past of a particular community that might have been inaccessible to the researcher. Oral tradition reveals the self-perception of communities, understanding about themselves. It helps to dig out how communities lived, their conflict, political authority/governance, social practices etc. It also provides glimpse into how people of the past constructed their words, idioms, metaphors, what they believed, imagined and valued. Oral tradition defines the sense of beauty and ugly, right and wrong, taboos, rites and rituals of a community. It provides worldview, creation story etc. From oral tradition the researcher is able to filter contemporary interpretations through the perception of community, interlocking in personal, social, political, economic and power relations of a community. The researcher may find conflicting and contesting accounts of events, perception and different opinion in the process of research, therefore, here cross examination of information would be required. At times establishing authenticity of accounts may become difficult.

6. Artefacts

Artefacts are tools, ornaments, cloth, weapons etc. created and used by a particular community, tribe or group for practical life in a particular period of time. It provides material evidence to the researcher of the economic, social, political and religious life of the community under study. It also sheds light on the civilization of a community of the past. It can provide historical, demographic and personal information about culture, society or people.

7. Written Documents

A researcher also can use written documents that already exist and can use as a part of research design. However, one has to be careful in the selection of written documents depending on the field or context of research. The written documents provide resources where direct and personal contact is impossible. The documents must be evaluated in conjunction with other evidence whether present new information or just conform to the already established pattern.

8. Audio-Video-Digital

As we are exposed to modern information technology, we can use modern gadgets as a method for our research. This method includes tape record, radio, picture, video, film, internet, email, WhatsApp etc. All these forms are expressed and reduced digitally. The collection of material can be done directly or indirectly. Now a days, this mechanical device is widely used. Through this method, research can be done faster and cheaper.

We cannot use one of these data collection methods exclusively for a given research project. We may have to use several of these methods together for data collection. The method of data collection will depend on the nature, design, and objectives of the research project.

Summary

This chapter highlighted various data collection methods, such as – interview, focus group, oral tradition/history, artefacts, written documents and audio-visual-digital. Interview method is a direct and primary method of data collection. There are three types of interview – structured interview with standardized questions, semi-structured interview both with and without standardized questions with flexibility and unstructured interview without standardized prepared questions. Focus group method is group discussion-based interview. This is qualitative research generated through group discussion, which requires a skilled moderator. Documentary method includes the life stories of an individual, group or community. Oral tradition/history is information of stories, histories, events, myth, and legends passed orally from generations to generations. Artefacts are tools, ornaments, cloth, weapons etc. which give information of a particular tribe or group of people for practical life in a particular time. Written documents are already written information of various subjects. Audio-video-digital method is tool that we can have information through modern technology and gadgets.

References

Burns, Robert B. *Research Methods.* New Delhi: SAGE Publications India Pvt. Ltd., 2000.

Finnegan, Ruth. "Using Documents." In *Data Collection and Analysis.* Edited by Ford, Roger Saps and Victor Jubb. New Delhi: SAGE Publications, 2006.

Giles-Vernick, Tamara. "Oral Histories as Methods and Sources." In *A Handbook for Social Science: Field Research.* Edited by Perelman, Ellen and Sara R. Curran. New Delhi: SAGE Publications, 2006.

Gosh, B. N. *Scientific Method and Social Research.* New Delhi: Sterling Publishers Private Limited, 1987.

Hill, Myrtle. "Focus Group." In *A-Z of Social Research.* Edited by Miller, Robert L. and John D. Brewer. New Delhi: SAGE Publications, 2007.

Lynne, J. Millard. "Focus Group." In *Research Methods in Psychology.* Edited by Breakwell, Glynis M. et.al. Singapore: SAGE Publications, 2007.

Morgan, David L. *Successful Focus Group: Advancing the State of the Art.* New Delhi: SAGE Publications, 1993.

O'Leary, Richard and Ciaran Acton. "Documentary Sources." In *The A-Z Social Research.* Edited by Miller, Robert E. and John D. Brewer. New Delhi: SAGE Publications, 2007.

Punch, Keith F. *Introduction to Social Research: Quantitative and Qualitative Approaches,* Second Edition. Los Angeles, London, New Delhi, Singapore: SAGE Publications, 2005.

Sapsford, Roger and Victor Juppe. *Data Collection and Analysis.* New Delhi: SAGE Publications, 2006.

Short, Susan E. "Focus Group Interview." In *A Handbook for Social Science Field Research.* Edited by Perelman, Ellen and Sara R. Curran. New Delhi: SAGE Publications India Pvt. Ltd., 2006.

Chapter 10

Case Study and Content Analysis

Introduction

Case Study and Content Analysis are other two methods of data collection. These methods are employed in many social science researches, including theological education. Case study and Content analysis are widely used in the field of Christian ministry, such as – Christian education, Counseling, Homiletics, and Communication. In this chapter we shall discuss about Case Study and Content Analysis methods.

1. Case Study: Meaning and Definition of Case Study

A case study is a detailed study of a single social unit. The social unit is usually located in one physical place, the people making social unit being differentiated from others who are not part of it. Case study is an intensive and purposive study of a case, which may be individual, an institution, a system, a community, an organization, an event, or even the entire culture. Fredrick Leplay was the first to introduce case study method in social research. Then, English social philosopher, Herbert Spencer was the first to use case study method in his comparative studies of different cultures. The case study method is used extensively in theological education, particularly in the Christian ministry (counselling and education) disciplines. This method has been used for education to develop developmental psychology and in counselling to develop clinical psychology. Sigmund Freud and Jean Piaget used case study method to develop their developmental theories. Anthropologists and ethnologists use case study method without unhinged. Historians also use this method in the study of secular history and history of Christianity to portray some historical character and historical development of a particular period of national community or church. It can be used either qualitatively or quantitatively or both but mainly used qualitatively. Despite heavy criticism, case study method is used extensively in qualitative research. The common critique against case study is that it is "catch-all" category that anything does not come under the purview of experimental, survey or historical method. Case study is a bounded system of research method.

Citing Queen, M. L. Sanghanam defines case study as "the examination of single situation, person, groups, or institution as complex whole in order to identify types and processes." Citing Schramm, Robert K. Yin defines case study that it is, "The essence of case study, the central tendency among all types of case study is that, it tries to illuminate a decision or set of decisions: why they were taken, how they were implemented, and with what result." According to Devendra Thakur "the term case study refers to a rather intensive examination of some single unit." The case study attempts to understand any research problem in a holistic or Gestaltist way. The aim of case study is to locate or identify the factors that account for the behaviour pattern of a given unit and its relationship with wider environment.

However, social scientists are not in unanimity in using case study in research project. Campbell and Stanley (1963), for example put forward objection by saying that "It seems well-nigh unethical at the present time to allow, as theses or dissertations case studies which involve a single group observed at one time only." On the other hand, Young (1956) supports case study by saying that "the most meaningful numerical studies in social science are those which are linked with exhaustive case studies describing accurately the inter-relationship of factors and processes."

1.1. Purpose of Case Study Method

Following Burns, Ram Ahuja proposes the purposes of case study as follows:

a. To use it as a preliminary to a major investigation as it may bring to light variables, processes and relationship that deserve more intensive investigation.
b. To prove the phenomenon deeply and analyse it intensively with a view to establish generalization about the wider population to which the unit belongs.
c. To get anecdotal evidence that illustrates more general findings.
d. To refute a universal generalization. A single case can represent a significant contribution to theory building and assist in focussing the direction of future investigation in the area.
e. To use it as a unique, typical and an interesting case in its own right.

1.2. Types of Case Study Method

a. Historical Case Studies

The historical case study traces the development of an organization/system over time. It can be used in the study of the growth and development of an organization, association, convention, synod etc. It can be done in many ways. If the life of an organization or association or synod is not so long, it may be done from the establishment of the organization or association and till date. However, if the history of particular association, convention or synod is too long, the researcher can take the case from a certain period. The historical case study is mostly done in historical studies. For example, a researcher may take the case of split of an association, organization, synod etc. It involves the development of an organization, institution or an association. Historical case study heavily relies on records, interviews and documents related to the particular organization. For this kind of research, the researcher must ensure that the necessary documents and records are available. If the researcher is not from the same organization, association or institution in order to have access to the information, he/she must avail due permission from the authorities. Some organization, institution or association may not be willing to grant access to the records and documents. In such case, the researcher has to explain the nature, purpose and objective of the research. In that case preliminary interview may be required.

b. Observational Case Studies

Observational case studies are carried out in a classroom situation in group of teachers or pupils or other groups. It uses variety of observation and interview methods as their major tools. Here the researcher is rarely total participant. Although, the observational case study is qualitative in nature, but its aim is to get the perspectives of the participants.

However, for the researcher, it is not always possible to remain detached from the investigation undertaken. The main focus in this case study, as suggested by Burns are a) a classroom or other specific place b) a group of people, such as choir group, teacher or students of a theological college and c) some activity of theological college, such as "graduation ceremony." A successful observational case study depends upon how the group is defined as a separate and distinct unit from general population. Participant observation is the usual technique in observational case study but the researcher has to ensure that there are sufficient numbers of people in a group. There is a danger in small group where participants may change their behaviour because of the presence of the researcher. Therefore, the researcher has to ensure that he/she has neutral effect in the research process. However, how a researcher is able to monitor his/her effect is a real challenge for the researcher.

c. Oral History Case Studies

These are usually first-person narratives that the researcher collects using extensive interviewing of a single individual. It is a first-person narrative that involves extensive interview of a single individual. For example, a study on blind children as seen and experienced by a teacher. It can be done, say on a retired theological teacher, his/her experiences or on a person of first-generation Christian to study spiritual growth or decline of his/her particular Christian community.

d. Situational Case Studies

This form of case study method studies particular events. Here the views of all participants in the event are sought. For example, study on the vandalism in school by students. In this situational case study students, teachers, eye witnesses and local magistrates will be extensively interviewed.

e. Clinical Case Studies

The aim of this approach is to understand in depth a particular individual such as – a patient in hospital, a prisoner in jail, a woman in a rescue home, a problem of a child in a school etc. These studies involve detailed interviews, observation, going through records and reports and so on.

f. Multi-case Studies

It is a collection of case studies or a form of replication, i.e., multiple experiments. This effort requires more and more effort.

1.3. Importance of Case Study Method

a. It is intensive in nature. In this method various aspects of a unit or a problem are studied.
b. Since this method is intensive in nature, it helps to gain knowledge. It enables to produce ideas, suggestions, hypotheses and behaviour.
c. It helps in formulating valid hypothesis, which helps to study the human nature and behaviour patterns intensively. After studying various aspects of life pattern, a researcher is able to formulate valid hypothesis.
d. It is a subjective study. So, it deals with the psychological aspects of human life. To eradicate social problem, this study is very essential.
e. It helps in framing questionnaire. The case study method is of immense help in framing questionnaire and schedules without which peculiarities and characteristics of the individual or group cannot be studied.

1.4. Distinctive Features of Case Study

a. Increase of knowledge: Since case study is done extensively on one particular single unit, there is possibility of increasing knowledge extensively in particular unit in depth.

b. Development of hypothesis: It leads to not only well 'established' conclusion but also to the development of empirical hypothesis.

c. Flexibility: In case study, the researcher has freedom in regards to the data collection, sources and procedures.

d. Application of troubled question: These days case study is done mostly for preventive measure rather than therapy, when a similar situation is broken. For example, in common occurrence of riot in India, the researcher tries to find out why it began. So, it is concerned with application of the case study in the study process of a situation of a problem.

1.5. Specific Steps in Case Study Approach

a. Determining status: The first step is to find out the descriptive information, the nature and extent of the problem to determine precisely the present status of the unit under investigation.

b. Gathering back information: The second step is to achieve an accurate description of the present situation; the researcher has collected as background data. Here the researcher collects information about the research problem and examine circumstances leading to the current crisis. At this point the researcher compiles reasonable list of possible causes of the present situation. He/she formulates the hypothesis about the true nature of the situation using the symptoms, which appear in the data.

c. Testing of hypothesis: By this time background information is obtained. After gathering background information, the researcher looks for specific relation to each of the hypothesis. The researcher tries to locate the various factors that influenced the individuals or the problem.
d. Instituting remedial action: The purpose of case study is to examine a problem of case intensively. In this step in the process of investigation, the researcher develops one or more hypotheses related to the original difficulties. This process is done by instituting some remedial or corrective measures and then examine what effect the change has brought out.

1.6. Planning the Case Study

Burns suggests that there are four components in planning the case study as follows:

a. Initial Case Study Questions

It deals with the question of who, what, where, when and how. For example, how and why theological colleges/seminaries cooperate and collaborate with one another to provide theological education.

b. Study Proposition

The question regarding who and why is not enough. It is vague unless it is expressed in proposition in succinct manner. So there has to be proposition of these who and why. For example, theological colleges/seminaries collaborate with one another to provide theological education because it is cheaper to run join courses.

c. Unit of Analysis

In this component the proposition of case study is narrowed down to certain specific issue. Here the focus is narrowed down and dealt with actual context, person, area, or event. For example, the unit of case study in theological education can be "women studies."

d. Linking Data to Propositions and Criteria for Interpreting Findings

The fourth component, according Burns is least developed and relates to the data analysis step.

1.7. Advantages and Disadvantages of Case Study

a. Advantages

i. It can offer insights for further research in large scale.
ii. Case study helps in adding more knowledge, ideas, suggestions and hypotheses about behaviour of individuals.
iii. It provides ideas about communities or categories of variables in exploring completely new fields.
iv. Unlike questionnaire and structured interview in case study, pertaining data related with a unit, organization and interaction with others are studied as a whole.
v. As case study is qualitative research, it is flexible in nature.

b. Disadvantages of Case Study Method

i. There is a chance of developing false confidence. There is a tendency that researcher may become over-confident. Since the views of various aspects of the life of an individual is taken into consideration, the researcher might think he/she knows everything about the person. But there will be hidden aspect in the life of an individual, which the respondent himself/herself was ignorant.

ii. There is difficulty in collecting historical data. Through this method, proper data collection is very difficult. This is because generally the respondents do not reveal the actual facts to the researchers. There is possibility of assumption all the past experiences or past happenings of an individual or community contributed to the final result.

iii. It is expensive in nature, considerable time and money is involved in the case study. Each case becomes a research in itself.

iv. While using personal letter and personal document, there is every possibility of distortion.

v. There is possibility of error in case study method. There can be many errors in selection of case observation due to shortage of memory, suspension of unpleasant facts, tendency to exaggerate and the like. As case study depends on retrospective data, there is possibility either to forget details of the data or purposefully falsify the data.

vi. The case study method is qualitative in nature. It only deals with psychological aspects of human being. Quantification of results is not possible in this type of study. So, there is lack of quantitative quality.

vii. Sometime it may be difficult for the researcher when to stop. It mainly depends on the recall of others past experiences and knowledge regarding past events.

viii. As case study often involves with case problem, there is tendency to overemphasize the undeserved traits and underestimate common desirable characteristics.

2. Content Analysis: Meaning and Definition

Content analysis is analysis of a text that can be in written forms, such as newspaper, articles, official and personal documents, books, pamphlets, tracts and the like, or accounts people proffer in interview and later described in written form. It can be undertaken quantitatively and qualitatively or both. The basic idea is to reduce the total content of communication to a set of categories that represent some characteristic of research interest. The researcher can take all of the words or all of the visual imaginary of the text. It involves systematic description of either verbal or nonverbal materials.

M. L. Sathanam and also P. G. George citing from Berelson, define, "Content analysis is a research technique for the objective, systematic, and quantitative description of the manifest content of communication." Kripperdorff defines content analysis as "a research technique for making replicable and valid inferences from data to their context." Paul V. Young cited by Sarabanal defines "Content analysis is a research technique for systematic, objective, and quantitative description of content of research procured through interviews, questionnaires, schedule and linguistic expressions, written or oral content." Holsti (1968) defines that "content analysis is any technique for making inferences by systematically and objectively identifying specific characteristics of messages." Kerlinger defines "Content analysis as a method of studying and analysing communication in a systematic, objective, and quantitative manner for the purpose of measuring variables."

Cohen defines content analysis simply, as the process of four "Cs", i.e., coding, categorising, comparing and concluding. He further states the following are the essential features of the process of content analysis:

a. Breaking down text into units of analysis.
b. Undertaking statistical analysis of the units.
c. Presenting the analysis in as economical form as possible.

The process of content analysis typically involves classifying or coding concepts, words and themes within content and analysing the results. Most importantly, in the process of content analysis it helps to quantify the occurrence of certain words, phrases, themes and concepts within the content.

2.1. A Brief Background of Content Analysis Method

Content analysis method as a social science research method took its inception during the time of World War II. The propaganda of second world war during war time propelled the emergence of content analysis method. The second world war took place between allied forces led by Britain, France and U.S. and German Nazi and Japan. During war time a lot of propagandas were propagated by both sides of the forces. So, the content analysis method was introduced to analyse the content of messages of enemies. Harold Laswell, an American sociologist can be considered pioneer in introducing this social method. Then Bernard Berelson expanded its use in social research. Berelson introduced content analysis as a versatile technique in communication and political research. In the 1940s content analysis method was mostly used in quantitative research. But by 1950s it was used mostly in qualitative research. However, content analysis can be used for both quantitative and qualitative research.

2.2. Objectives of Content Analysis Method

The objective of content analysis method is to 'read between the lines.' It aims to determine answers to questions where the text implies something and is not necessarily explicit.

Content analysis is research that can analyse human communications, how people plan their lives, what people know about something, and how people react to something. The objective of content analysis is to transform recorded 'raw' phenomena into data that can be processed scientifically in nature so that a body of knowledge can be constructed. In fact, a researcher wishing to conduct a content analysis study must next address four methodological issues. Selection of units of analysis, development of categories, selection of appropriate content, verification of coding reliability. We can also say that the objective of content analysis is to simplify complex, unstructured content, identify content trends, patterns and relationships, determining content properties, analyse content to identify personal intent and identifying the aspects of content.

Citing Berelson, Ahuja provides five procedures in determining the objectivity of content analysis as follows:

a. Rule-guided Procedure

In content analysis strict adherents to rule-guided procedure is given importance.

In content analysis, the researcher is more concerned with the establishment of rules and methods than the creation of categories to analyse the content of materials. Nor the researcher give priority in the classification of units of communication.

b. Systematic Procedure

It is not only rule-based enforcement, but the researcher has to pay attention to systematic approach to contribute to the objectivity of content analysis. For example, if a researcher wants to compare news and editorials in several newspapers to analyse gang violence in a city, the researcher has to make a valid comparison of materials under study. The researcher has to follow systematic procedure when documenting the content of individual newspapers.

c. Quantitative Description

It is important to count the frequency of publication in various newspapers, magazines and correspondences and compare their relevance. Its aim is to assess the strength of a particular variable. For example, if a researcher wants to compare the attitudes of the principals of 10 theological colleges under the Senate of Serampore College (University) and their opinion on various aspects of the theological education system, a comparison of attitudes and opinion is only possible if positive and negative comments are recorded quantitatively. This is different from a simple frequency measurement.

d. Focus on Qualitative Analysis

As content analysis is done both qualitatively and quantitatively, focusing solely on frequency counts when analysing content analysis will not suffice. It will not help in obtaining accurate meaning of communication. Therefore, both quantitative and qualitative techniques should be used with one another.

e. Assessing only the Manifest Content Communication

In any content analysis, there will be both overt and covert or explicit and implicit messages. The researcher while doing content analysis needs to pay attention to both aspects. Therefore, researchers need to "read between the lines" to make sense of what is perceived. Without this, it affects the objectivity of the analysis. Therefore, we should not only focus on what is explicitly manifested in communication but also the implicit contents that lie quiescently beneath the surface.

2.3. Purpose of Content Analysis

Content analysis is a systematic coding and categorizing approach, which one can use unobtrusively to explore large amounts of textual information in-order to ascertain the trends and patterns of words used, their frequency, their relationships and the structures and discourses of communication. One can use this approach to analyse media and policy documents, visual images and actions, medical and other personal records, speeches and transcripts.

The ultimate purpose of content analysis is to help the testing of hypothesis by providing necessary quantitative data. Content analysis provides definite and objective answer in lieu of judgments or impressions. The analysis needs to be objective and systematic, and lead to more reliable results. Its aim is to develop an elaborate technique for the quantification of materials and thereby help the proper coding of data. According to L. Festinger and Daniel Katz, content analysis aims at converting recorded raw phenomena into data which can be treated essentially in a scientific manner so that a system of knowledge may be built up. Content analysis can create reproducible or objective data which can be quantitatively measured and which can be significant for scientific theorizing.

Berelson (1952) provides the following purposes for content analysis:

a. To disclose the international differences in communication content.
b. To compare media or "levels" of communication.
c. To audit communication content against objectives.
d. To codify open-ended questions in surveys.
e. To identify the intentions and other characteristics of the communicator.

f. To determine the psychological state of persons or groups.
g. To detect the existence of propaganda.
h. To describe attitudinal and behavioural responses to communications.
i. To reflect cultural patterns of groups, institutions, or societies.
j. To reveal the focus of individual, group, institutional, or societal attention.
k. To describe the trends in communication content.

Further, the followings can be identified as purpose of content analysis.

a. To identify the motive of the communicator(s).
b. To detect the existence of propaganda.
c. To obtain political intelligence.
d. To identify psychological attitudes.
e. To propagate or destroy value, system or attitude.
f. To describe attitudinal and behavioural response of the communicator(s).
g. To describe the communication trends.
h. To trace the development of ideas or theories or empirical facts.
i. To compare different communication system or agents.
j. To help in research.

2.4. Use of Content Analysis

The first main use of content analysis in social research was in the immediate period after the Second World War when American sociologists used it to quantitatively and systematically to describe and analyse the content of communications containing propaganda.

Though scholars from various disciplines such as social sciences, communications, psychology, political science, history, and language studies use content analysis, it is most widely used in social science and mass communication research. It has been used broadly to understand a wide range of themes such as social change, cultural symbols, changing trends in the theoretical content of different disciplines, verification of authorship, changes in the mass media content, nature of news coverage of social issues or social problems such as atrocities against women, dowry harassment, social movements, ascertaining trends in propaganda, election issues as reflected in the mass media content, and so on.

One of the most frequent uses of the content analysis is to study the changing trends in the theoretical content and methodological approaches by content, analysing the journal articles of the discipline (Loy, 1979). Using this approach, Vijayalakshmi analysed a stratified random sample of 194 research articles published in the *Indian Journal of Social Work* from 1971 to 1990 to identify characteristics of authors, and document, the trends in empirical content, subject areas, and methodological characteristics such as source of data, research design, sampling, and statistical techniques used in the articles. Similarly, public attitude towards important issues such as civic amenities, unemployment and so on were assessed by analysing the content of editorials or letters to the editor in newspapers. One significant area of its use has been the analysis of newspaper content of the election coverage and editorial treatment to mould the opinion of voters. For example, Devi Prasad analysed the editorials and letters to the editor published in four *Dailies* in India before the 1991 elections to find out the prominent election related themes which figured in the news and direction of their coverage in the respective newspapers.

Researchers use content analysis to find out about the purposes, messages, and effects of communication content. They also can make inferences about the producers and audience of the texts they analyse.

In addition, content analysis can be used to make qualitative inferences by analysing the meaning and semantic relationship of words and concepts. Because content analysis can be applied to a broad range of texts. It can be used in a variety of fields, including marketing, media studies, anthropology, cognitive science, psychology, and many social science disciplines.

Currently content analysis is also used in different fields, ranging from marketing and media studies, to literature and rhetoric, ethnography and cultural studies, gender and age issues, sociology and political science, psychology and cognitive science, and many other fields of inquiry. Berelson offers the following list for more possibilities in the use of content analysis:

a. Revelation of international differences in communication content.
b. Detection of the existence of propaganda.
c. Identification of the intentions, focus or communication trends of an individual, group or institution.
d. Description of attitudinal and behavioural responses to communications.
e. In determining psychological or emotional state of persons or groups.

Content analysis can be used to study the attitudes of persons or the press on certain important issues, such as – racial prejudice, prohibition, international relations, development policy. The speeches and propaganda of politicians and diplomats can be subjected to content analysis. R. K. White's content analysis of the public speeches of Hitler and Roosevelt revealed that these two leaders appealed to the public by means of the references of three values—strength values, economic values and moral values. Content analysis can be applied to analyse any piece of content that is written or verbal. Content analysis is involved in a variety of fields such as politics, human behaviour, marketing, literature, health, psychology, and much more. Content analysis is also used in theological education, particularly Christian education (to analyse content of curriculum), pastoral counselling, homiletics etc. Content analysis also displays a close relation between the linguistic factors and psychological aspects, thereby leading to the study of Artificial Intelligence (AI).

2.5. Types of Content Analysis

Primarily, content analysis had been used as a quantitative research method. But now, it is used both in qualitative and quantitative research. The qualitative approach of this technique has been able to address key areas of the quantitative approach. Therefore, now instead of a single content analysis, there are three different approaches – conventional, directed and summative.

In terms of types, there are generally two types of content analysis: Quantitative or Conceptual Analysis and Qualitative or Relational Analysis: However, they are diversified.

a. Quantitative or Conceptual Analysis

Traditionally, content analysis has most often been thought of in terms of quantitative analysis. In quantitative or conceptual analysis, a concept is chosen for examination, and the analysis involves quantifying and tallying its presence, which is also known as thematic analysis. The focus here is on looking at the occurrence of selected terms within a text, the term could be found as synonyms (explicit) or as a concept using a cluster of different words (implicit). The identification of the second category is little difficult.

Quantitative or Conceptual analysis begins with identifying research questions and choosing a sample or samples. In the sample, text is sought and put in the different categories or the content is codified in different categories. This method is known as selective reduction. By reducing the text to categories consisting of a word, set of words or phrases, the researcher can focus on, and code for, specific words or patterns that are indicative of the research question.

Typically, people think of conceptual analysis when they think of content analysis. In conceptual analysis, a concept is chosen for examination and the analysis involves quantifying and counting its presence. The main goal is to examine the occurrence of selected terms in the data. Terms may be explicit or implicit. Explicit terms are easy to identify. Coding of implicit terms is more complicated: one needs to decide the level of implication and base judgments on subjectivity (an issue for reliability and validity). Therefore, coding of implicit terms involves using a dictionary or contextual translation rules or both.

To begin a conceptual content analysis, first the researcher needs to identify the research question and choose a sample or samples for analysis. Next, the text must be coded into manageable content categories. This is basically a process of selective reduction. By reducing the text to categories, the researcher can focus on and code for specific words or patterns that inform the research question.

Quantitative content analysis generates numerical values from the verbatim text. However, the process by which these values are generated may include elements of qualitative analysis, making the qualitative-quantitative distinction far from clear-cut. Quantitative content analysis is slightly mislabelled anyway, as it is less a type of analysis than a way of producing data which can then be statistically analysed, i.e., the output of the content analysis is not the end of the analysis as a whole.

b. Qualitative or Relational Analysis

Relational analysis begins like conceptual analysis, where a concept is chosen for examination. However, the analysis involves exploring the relationships between concepts. Individual concepts are viewed as having no inherent meaning and rather the meaning is a product of the relationships among concepts.

Even to begin with a relational content analysis, the researcher, first one needs to identify a research question and choose a sample or samples for analysis. The research question must be focused so that concept types are not open to interpretation and can be summarized. Then next step is selection of text for analysis. The researcher needs to select the text for analysis carefully by balancing having enough information for a thorough analysis so that results are not limited with having information that is too extensive so that the coding process becomes too arduous and heavy to supply meaningful and worthwhile results.

There are three subcategories of relational analysis to choose from prior to going on to the general steps are as follows:

i. Affect Extraction

Affect Extraction is emotional evaluation of concepts explicit in a text. A challenge to this method is that emotions can vary across time, populations, and space. However, it could be effective at capturing emotional and psychological state of the speaker or writer of the text.

ii. Proximity Analysis

Proximity Analysis is evaluation of the co-occurrence of explicit concepts in the text. Text is defined as a string of words called a "window" that is scanned for the co-occurrence of concepts. The result is the creation of a "concept matrix," or a group of interrelated co-occurring concepts that would suggest an overall meaning.

iii. Cognitive Mapping

Cognitive mapping is visualization technique for either affect extraction or proximity analysis. Cognitive mapping attempts to create a model of the overall meaning of the text such as a graphic map that represents the relationships between concepts.

Qualitative or Relational Analysis is an extension to the quantitative analysis. However, qualitative analysis seeks to go beyond presence of concepts by exploring the relationships between the concepts identified. Relational analysis has also been termed as semantic analysis. In other words, the focus of relational analysis is to look for semantic, or meaningful relationships. Individual concepts are viewed as having no inherent meaning. Rather, meaning is a product of the relationships among concepts in a text.

Basically, there are two key theoretical approaches for qualitative content analysis – linguistics and cognitive science.

a. Linguistics

Linguistic approach to content analysis focuses on the analysis of texts on the level of a linguistic unit, typically single clause units. One example of this type of research is

Gottschalk (1995), who developed an automated procedure, which analyses each clause in a text and assigns it a numerical score based on several emotional/psychological scales.

b. Cognitive Science

Cognitive science approaches include the creation of decision maps and mental models. Decision maps attempt to represent the relationship(s) between ideas, beliefs, attitudes, and information available to an author when deciding within a text. These relationships can be represented as logical, inferential, causal, sequential, and mathematical relationships. Typically, two - of these links are compared in a single study, and are analysed as networks. This methodology is thought of as a more generalized cognitive mapping technique, rather than the more specific mental model's approach.

2.6. Diversified Types of Content Analysis

a. Descriptive analysis: Descriptive analysis means counting the frequency in appearance of certain elements of the research question and comparing it with other elements.
b. Categorical analysis: In it, analysis involves a study of the documents by means of a set of categories, producing nominal as well as ordinal and interval data, which are then processed statistically.
c. Intensity analysis: In this type content is processed by means of multi-step scales based on theoretical criteria.
d. Contingency analysis: It is basically a systematic analysis that is usually employed to make an inference from text about the personality of the author.
e. Contextual analysis: In this type the sequence in which concepts appear to gather is examined. The

systematic appearance is not considered accidental, but it expresses the thinking pattern of the author.

2.7. Process of Content Analysis

The process of content analysis is to systematically analyse and interpret the content of various forms of communication such as written, oral and visual in order to identify patterns, themes and meanings. The research through content analysis involves four processes. They are discussed briefly here under:

a. Specifying the Problem

It aims to identify specific research questions in the chosen problem. For example, "Caste violence in Bihar" suggested by Ahuja, the following research questions can be asked: (a) Which "Senna" are formed by different lower or upper castes? (b) What are the prominent castes? (c) What are the main causes of violence? (d) What geographic regions are they concentrated in? (e) How many massacres have occurred in recent years? (f) What political parties do the different castes support? It must be theoretically identified in terms of theories such as violence, political behaviour, caste interdependence, establishment of caste-based ministries, and caste-based vote searches. Logically, this brings the researcher's attention to the nature of the data source, i.e., books and magazines dealing with subjects such as Indian caste and politics, mob violence, police and violence. These books and journals offer researchers the opportunity to conduct more thorough comparative and theoretical analysis than the data sources allow.

b. Sampling

By sampling here refers to sampling of newspapers, magazines, books, TV dramas, songs, novels, etc. A sampling of books refers to a sampling of old and new books and popular magazines known for their analytical views. For example, on the topic of caste violence in Bihar one can see magazines such as 'India Today', 'The Week', 'Outlook', 'Frontline', 'Seminar' and 'Business and Political Weekly.' Sampling also requires sampling items for analysis. When the total number of items to be analysed is large, researchers need to focus on relevant and meaningful items and include a large number of communication materials in the analysis.

c. Choosing Units of Analysis

Gardner has pointed out the following units of analysis:

i. The single word: It is often used in psychotherapy research and literary renditions.
ii. The theme of subject, e.g., propaganda, advertisement, values, attitudes, violence, etc.
iii. The character, i.e., socio-economic marital status, psychological traits, and other personality traits. This is commonly used in mass media research (film, television, etc.).
iv. The sentence or the paragraph: This is more likely to be used with mass media data, which consists a lot of data.
v. The item, i.e., the entire book, film, article, or radio programme is characterised.
vi. The context units.

d. Category Construction

It categorizes the content of the materials considered. The categories constructed should reflect the main theoretical concepts underlying the research. Following types of categories used in content analysis research are suggested by Berelson:

i. Subject matter: What is the communication about?
ii. Direction: How is the subject matter treated?
iii. Standard: What are the criteria for classification?
iv. Values: What values and goals are revealed?
v. Methods: What means are used to achieve goals?
vi. Traits: What characteristics are used to describe people?
vii. Actor: Who is represented in taking specific actions?
viii. Authority: In whose name are statements made?
ix. Origin: Where does the communication originate?
x. Target: To what persons or groups is the communication directed?
xi. Location: Where does the action take place?
xii. Conflict: What are the sources and levels of conflict?
xiii. Time: When does the action take place?

2.8. Importance of Content Analysis Method

a. One of the significant advantages of content analysis is that, it is thoroughly unobtrusive method, i.e., no effect on the subject being studied.
b. It makes possible a variety of cross-cultural studies that would likely be unfeasible using other methods.
c. It can be used to test preliminary ideas, hypotheses or theories prior to more complete investigation.
d. It is a powerful tool for evaluating personal or social values.
e. This method is more useful where research budget is small and resources are limited.

2.9. Limitations of Content Analysis Method

a. Some content analysis is a heavily planned, it lacks the spontaneity and unplanned qualities of field research.
b. Determining validity is rather difficult. For example, in workers strike, whether or not newspapers gave the real feelings and the values of the worker.
c. Some required documents may not be available to the researcher which may affect the conclusion.
d. It is susceptible to coder bias.

2.10. Advantages and Disadvantages of Content Analysis

Followings are some advantages and disadvantages of content analysis:

a. Advantages

First, a major advantage of content analysis is that it is unobtrusive. A researcher can "observe" without being observed, since the contents being analysed are not influenced by the researcher's presence. Information that might be difficult, or even impossible, to obtain through direct observation or other means can be gained unobtrusively through analysis of textbooks and other communications, without the author or publisher being aware that it is being examined.

Second the advantage of content analysis is that it is extremely useful as a means of analysing interview and observational data. A third advantage of content analysis is that the researcher can delve into records and documents to get some feel for the social life of an earlier time. He or she is not limited by time and space to the study of present events. A fourth advantage accrues from the fact that the logistics of content analysis are often relatively simple and economical—

with regard to both time and resources—as compared to other research methods. This is particularly true if the information is readily accessible, as in newspapers, reports, books, periodicals, and the like. Finally, because the data are readily available and almost always can be returned to if necessary or desired, content analysis permits replication of a study by other researchers. Even live television programmes can be recorded for repeated analysis at later times.

b. Disadvantages

i. It can be criticized for being too positivist in orientation, particularly when only enumerative approaches are used.
ii. It can end up focusing only on word counts, leaving no possibility of more detailed interpretations.
iii. It can decontextualize information.
iv. It can often be a theoretical, with minimal interpretation, on the assumption that numbers say it all.
v. It takes time to be done.
vi. Relational analysis is a matter of high interpretation, hence is prone to inaccuracy.
vii. It is based on few steps; there is no sound theory to date, behind doing content analysis, which may reduce the precision of study sometimes.
viii. In content analysis a large concept is reduced to a code. Often there can be mistakes while coding, particularly dealing with complex texts and can result in 'information loss'.
ix. Often content analysis is criticized to be as word count.

x. Often we need to understand the context while drawing a conclusion from an analysed text because there could be many possible interpretations.

Summary

Case study and content analysis are two methods that are widely used in social research. Both methods are primarily qualitative research. There are six types of case study, such as – historical case study, observational case study, oral history case study, situational case study, clinical case study and multi-case study. Distinctive features of case study are – increase of knowledge, development of hypothesis, flexibility, application of troubled questions. Determining status, gathering back information, testing hypothesis and instituting remedial action are the steps of case study. The objective of case study is to "read in between the lines."

There are mainly two types of content analysis – Quantitative or conceptual and qualitative or relational. Qualitative relational has three subcategories – affect extraction, proximity analysis and cognitive mapping. It has two theoretical approaches, namely – linguistic and cognitive science. The process of content analysis is – specifying the problem, sampling, choosing unit of analysis and category construction.

References

Ahuja, Ram. *Research Methods*. Jaipur: Rawat Publications, 2011.

Brewer, John. "Content Analysis." In *The A-Z of Social Research*. Edited by Robert L. Miller and John D. Brewer. New Delhi: SAGE Publications, 2007.

George, P. G. *Scientific Method and Social Research*. New Delhi: Sterling Publishers Pvt. Ltd., 1992.

Ghosh, B. N. *Scientific Method and Social Research*. 4th edition, New Delhi: Sterling Publishers Private Limited, 2011.

Goode, William J. and Paul K. Hutt. *Methods in Social Research.* Delhi: Surjeet Publications, 2006.

Holsti, O. R. "Content Analysis" in G. Lindzey and E. Aronson (Eds.). *The Handbook of Social Psychology,* 2nd edition, Vol. II. New Delhi: Amerind Publishing Co., 1968.

Kerlinger, F. N. *Foundations of Research Method,* 3rd edition. London: SAGE Publications, 1980.

Payne, Geoff and Juy Payne. *Key Concept in Social Research.* New Delhi: SAGE Publications, 2006.

Singleton, Royce A. and Bruce C. Straits. *Approach to Social Research.* 3rd edition, New York: Oxford University Press, 1999.

Sarabanal, P. *Research Methodology.* Allahabad: Kitab Mahal, 2006.

Thakur, Devendra. *Research Methodology in Social Science.* New Delhi: Deep and Deep Publications Pvt. Ltd., 2008.

Yin, Robert K. *Case Study Research Design and Methods.* 3rd edition, New Delhi: SAGE Publications, Inc, 2003.

Chapter 11

Analysis of Case Materials and Documents

Introduction

In this chapter we shall discuss in brief how to use and collect data in social research through analysis of case materials, personal document, document relating to institutions, community, political parties and other agencies. These are very important sources of data collection in social research. Especially, sources relating to institutions, community, and organizations, such as church, association, convention, synod etc. are very important and useful materials in theological research for theological education.

1. Analysis of Case Materials

Case materials are relevant for the social scientists, who employ not only logico-deductive method, discovery and induction but also certain logical systems that do not fit into traditional categories of scientific inquiry as formulated by philosophers of science. Even social scientists committed to statistical hypothesis must rely upon case materials as a basis for understanding. One of the reasons sociologists are often unaware of the critical role of case materials for interpreting data is that they tend to carry out research only within their own society and moreover rely upon their own personal experience as case data to provide the contextual basis for interpreting their own findings. Even if a social scientist study cultural divergent from their own, they become more aware of the role of case materials, whether normal or deviant, or extreme, in the interpretation of tabular data.

1.1. Personal Documents

Personal documents are those documents, where necessary information is collected from the personal diaries, letters or autobiographies. Personal diaries provide information not only of the persons but various events related to the persons of that period. The study through personal diary is an interactive method, where the writer has more control over information than in an interview. In this study, the researcher has freedom to record what he/she wishes to record in it. Therefore, personal documents are and can be used as a source of information. If the person is still alive due permission is required.

2. Documents Relating to Institutions

2.1. School as a Source of Community-Based Studies

Schools and colleges can be used as a source for local community-based studies in two particular ways: a) It can be used as a forum to identify the key informants about the community b) it can be used as a basis for deriving a sample for further study of some aspects of its development.

Schools are generally viewed by the communities as an important and key figure in the community, even in government officials, businessmen and women, and also by the elders of the society. Schools maintain up to date information, such as – names of students, date of enrolment, year of admission, graduation etc. Some information may be found even in the archive. Therefore, if a researcher studies about an individual or the community, schools can provide necessary information about an individual.

2.2. Schools for Education Research

Schools can be place of information of primary sources for research in education. Schools provide primary data of school studies on learning and achievement, curriculum, learning, materials, aspirations, expectation of the students, performance of the teachers, environment of the school etc. Beside these, the secondary data comprises not only the statistical data on the enrolment and attendance, teachers' qualifications and performances of examination, but also learning materials, buildings and infrastructure. To conduct research through questionnaire, permission is required from school authorities and from the board of management by giving the view of the questionnaire in advance.

The researcher can have direct access to data through facilitating and informants of the institution. The immediate identification with the students, teachers and the community at large of the school, place the researcher in the context to which the subjects of the research can be related to. It will give the researcher a better sense of his/her personality and also the sense of active contributor to the life of the community.

3. Community

To analyse and understand the community, its environment and factors have to be considered. We can categorize the study of community into two: Urban and Rural. They have different set up that constitute urban and rural community.

A researcher must observe the differences between urban and rural communities.

3.1. Urban Community

In urban, physical environment influences the community. The layout of streets, buildings, transportation and other amenities influence the human habitat of urban community. All physical mechanism and technical devices have a definite relationship to social purposes and problems in urban community. Therefore, the researcher should know how human needs and social organization fit into the structural pattern of the community. Generally, urban area is an industrialized area and it affects the life style, thought pattern and social fabric of the community. The researcher should be broadly conscious of the nature and significance of the local government, the local educational system, the religious organization and the types of social welfare that influence the community.

3.2. Rural Community

In rural community research, the researchers do not necessarily need new sets of tools when they move from an urban to a rural environment. Some of the principles and methods of scientific inquiry applied in urban research can be applied in rural area too. As far as physical feature is concerned rural areas are less densely populated, generally more homogeneous, less mobile and not so highly stratified. In general, social interaction in rural community is more intimate, social control is largely persuasive, behaviour is closely regulated by the mores and folkways; and the status tends to be assigned in relation to the whole personality rather than on the basis of segmented role. Rural community poses challenges for the researcher, but in certain cases it can be simpler than the urban research.

3.3. Compare and Contrast of Urban and Rural Communities in Research

a. The Sources of Data

The sources of data in rural areas are generally more limited than in urban areas. Records, reports, and other sources of secondary information are scare in rural communities. Therefore, the researcher must depend upon unprofessional and untrained informants.

b. The Context of the Research

The context of social research in rural communities also differs in some respects from the subject matter usually analysed in urban areas. In urban area, communities are economically industrial driven, but rural areas economy is agro-based, so there is deeper relationship between human and land, farm income, tenancy etc. Therefore, the researcher should be concerned with health, diet, sanitation, education, social security and conservation of land on rural area in his/her research.

3.4. Objectives in Rural Development

The researchers can have some definite objectives in their research for rural development, such as – 1) raising the standard of living of people, 2) alleviating poverty in rural areas and improving the quality of life, 3) development both in farming and non-farming activities so as to generate gainful employment, 4) to change the attitudes of the rural people towards transformation of village community, 5) provision of social infrastructure, such as drinking water, health care, education, sanitation, housing, road, electrification etc. and 6) maximum utilization of local resources without adversely affecting the environment.

4. Organizations

4.1. Non-Government Organizations (NGOs)

Non-governmental organization refers to an organization which operates on a scale larger than the community. It is non-profit organization and citizen based. It covers a whole range of types of organization – international NGO, national NGO, local community-based organization (CBO), religious groups and social movements. The NGOs are registered body and have salaried staff with at least through one source of funding, but CBOs are likely operated at a smaller scale with or without funding. In most studies of NGOs, qualitative method is used for research, but in some cases quantitative method also can be employed. Some of the methods that can be employed are: 1) interview with key informants, such as NGO staff and project leaders, 2) focus group discussion, 3) surveys in the project location, 4) participatory appraisal with beneficiaries 5) document analysis of NGOs reports and baseline surveys.

4.2. Research on Non-NGOs

In certain studies, research question may not be directly related to issues about NGOs, but we may nevertheless find them useful resources of information for the research. The NGO staff can be informants and CBO leaders can act as representatives, particularly in places where there are only few institutions. The data collected by the NGO, for example on local, social, economic and environmental conditions will be useful for a range of research topic.

5. Political Parties

Political parties are formal organization for representing the aims and interest of different socio-economic forces in the political parties. It is an organizational means by which candidates are recruited for office and ideologies are propagated. The political party which runs the government is called ruling party. When more than two political parties are actively involved in politics, the system is called multi-party-political system. Indian political system is a multi-party-political system. When two or more than two political parties run the government, it is called coalition-government, such as BJP lead NDA (National Democratic Alliance) government at the centre in India. There are various national (INC, BJP) and regional (AGP, BSP, AIDMK, DMK etc.) political parties in India.

5.1. Analysis of Political Party Document

In order to carry out research on political parties, it requires the analysis of the documents of the particular political party, such as – formation of the party, constitution of the party, rules and regulation, the manifesto, the strategic plan, and also in some cases election platform as well as the party leaders and membership list. Party documents of material relevant to the research should be obtained from the party office through the secretaries or registrar of the party. The scope of analysis should focus on the party's origin or formation, the objectives, the policy, strategies and framework. Also, the following points should be considered – 1) the failure and success of the party from its inception, 2) its contribution for the welfare and development of society, 3) the position and condition of the party in the contemporary political system and governing.

Summary

Case materials are relevant for the scientists, who employ not only logico-deductive method but also certain logical system in the research project. Personal documents are those documents, where necessary information can be collected from personal diaries, letters, and biographies.

Documents relating to institutions like schools provide up to date information, such as – name of students, date of enrolment, year of admission, graduation etc. for research on institutions. Community, rural or urban is another source of research in the study of development, needs, problems, issues etc. of communities. NGOs and political parties are sources of research on certain NGOs and political parties.

References

Ahuja, Ram. *Research Methods.* Jaipur: Rawat Publications, 2011.

Gosh, B. N. *Scientific Methods & Social Research.* Delhi: Sterling Publishers Private Limited, 1982.

Gould, Bill. "Working with Partners: Educational Institutions." In *Doing Development Research.* Edited by Vandana Desai and Robert B. Potter. New Delhi: SAGE Publications, 2006.

Gregor, JoAnn Mc. "Diaries and Case Studies." In *Doing Development Research.* Edited by Vandana Desai and Robert B. Potter. New Delhi: SAGE Publications, 2006.

Marshal, Gordon. *A Dictionary of Sociology.* New York: Oxford University Press, 1994.

Mercer, Claire. "Doing with Partners." In *Doing Development Research.* Edited by Vandana Desai and Robert B. Potter. New Delhi: SAGE Publications, 2006.

Chapter 12

Tabulation, Analysis and Interpretation

Introduction

In the previous chapters we have discussed various methods of data collection process. Once the data are collected by various data collection methods for a given research project the next step is to tabulate, analyse and interpret the data collected. Without tabulation, analysis and interpretation data will remain mere numbers. It will not bear any meaning. Without purpose and significance data will remain as bare skeleton. This step of research is very crucial even in theological education, particularly in the discipline of Christian ministry. Data is to support the research empirically and tabulation, analysis and interpretation are to give meaning and significance of the research undertaken. This chapter will deal with tabulation, analysis and interpretation of data in the research project.

1. Tabulation

Tabulation is an essential part of a research project and a technical process in the statistical data analysis. The main purpose of tabulation in research project is to determine the number of cases that fall into various categories. Tabulation is done by arranging data in orderly form into series of rows and columns. This will help read the data in two dimensions. Through tabulation the researcher can present particular result of the inquiry or investigation undertaken. Unless the data are properly classified in the table "the raw" material will mean nothing. It will not have any meaning and significance. The researcher will not be able to come to conclusion or find solution to any problem. Tabulation is a process of representation. The reason or significance are:

a. It helps in simplifying the comparison of data.
b. It makes the study complete and accurate in every aspect.
c. It makes the comparison of data easier and saves a lot of time and energy.
d. It provides possibility to make statistical treatment.

2. Charts

Charts serve to present graphic presentation of data that transform data into components. We can see the data in visual form from large and complex sets of data into simple form. Chart makes data visually organized and present people to understand and connect with the possible conclusion drawn from data analysis. They are made up of symbols, shapes, and notations that help to navigate and interpret data easily that is being presented. There are different types of charts as discussed below:

2.1. Pie Chart

Pie chart is formed in circle with each category occupying a segment that is proportionate in size. It is a circular graph that shows numerical data as a percentage of a whole. Pie chart is made of slice or "pie," for example, an apple pie, that represent different categories. The total value of pie is always 100%. The total sum of data in pie chart is always 360 degree. There are different types of pie charts, such as – Doughnut pie chart, with a whole in the centre. Exploded pie chart, where one or more slices are separated from the rest of the pie to emphasize them and then Nested pie chart, also known as multilevel or hierarchical pie chart. To calculate the percentage of data the formula used is (Frequency divided by total value of data into 100).

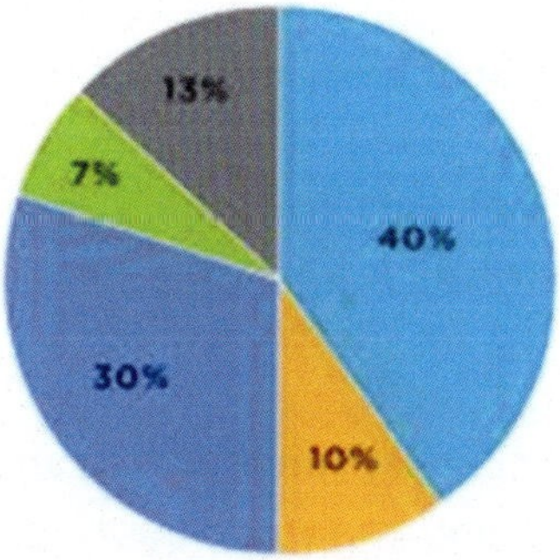

Pie Chart

2.2. Stacked Bar Chart

The stacked bar chart has two bar and each bar shows information about two or more variables staked into each other vertically. The various sections of the bar show the proportion of variables they represent in relation to each other. It is a graph related values stacked on top to each other. Each bar is made of sub-bar. Negative values are stacked in reverse order. Stacked bars charts are used when a category naturally divides into components.

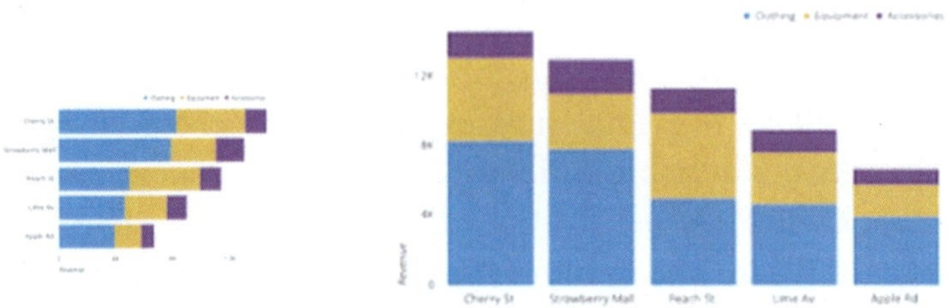

Stacked Bar Chart

3. Diagram

In certain research work, the researcher has to use large mass of data or universe in statistical methods and other allied subjects. In such case, difficulty may arise when mass data have to be tabulated. Hence, there arise the need of diagram to represent data in a simplified manner collected in the research process. The diagrammatic and graphical representation help to understand and remember data in easy way for a long time. There are some factors we need to consider before we choose suitable diagram as follows:

a. Selection of Diagram: Before drawing actual diagram there has to be definite and tentative selection of the diagram. One should not rush to draw diagram without proper consideration.
b. Suitable Title: Any diagram without proper and suitable title often will fail to attract the attention of the reader.
c. Size and Appearance: Another prerequisite is the adjudgment of its nature, type and size. For example, diagram should not be too large or too small that lose its genuineness and importance.
d. Neatness: We must keep in mind that diagrams must be neat and clean that will attract readers and achieve their objective. Therefore, before selection of diagram

the researcher must consider all the factors that may hinder attention of the readers. The diagram should not be too colourful or artistic, otherwise it will fail to achieve its goal.

e. Comparability: The task of diagram is not only to represent statistical data and information, but also to make comparison between two or more tables or statistical data and information. Therefore, to represent reliable and authentic data there has to be possibility of making comparison of different diagram. If there is possibility of comparison of diagram, there will be greater utility and significance.

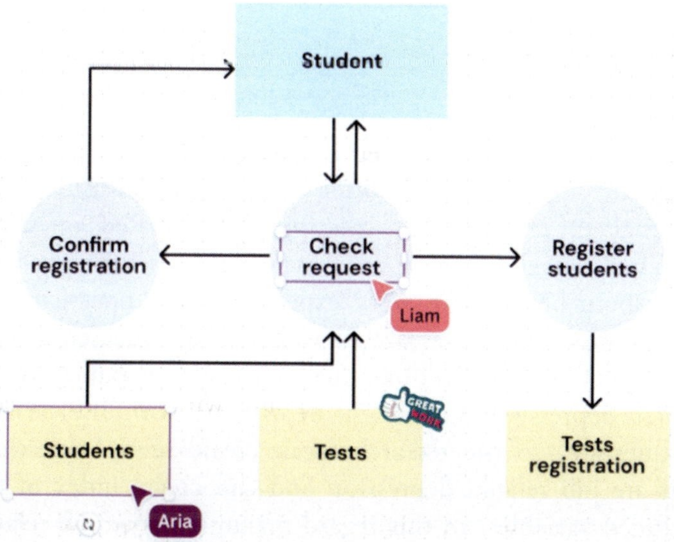

Data Flow Diagram (DFD)

4. Figure

Figures provide powerful visual presentation and they are effective tool for research work. Figures communicate trends or relationship and general pattern emerging from database.

They are also used to present complex data in simple form. Figures are presented in various form, such as – graphs, drawing, maps and photos. The researcher must know how to present figures in a given research. There are certain core elements by which figures can be presented as follows: 1) Title: Every figure must have a title that is clear and concise and must summarize the main points of presented data. The numbering of figure must be sequential and must correspond to the reference provided in the text. 2) Type of figure: The type of figure to be used usually dictated by the kind of information it wants to convey. 3) Use of image: While using figures the researcher must ensure they are of high resolution, which are clear and sharp.

5. Index and Scale

5.1. Index

Indexes help the researcher in quantitative social science research, because they offer composite measure that summarizes response for multiple rank related questions or statements. This composite measure gives the researcher data about belief, attitude or experience of the participants. For example, if the researcher wants to do research on the interest of job satisfaction, one of the key variables is job related depression. This might be difficult with one variable or question, so the researcher can create several questions that are job related depression and can create index of the included variables. In this regard maximum four job related questions can be asked with "yes" or "no" response.

5.2. Scale

A scale is composite measure that is composed of several items. These items have logical and empirical structure among them. Scale takes advantage of differences in intensity among the indicators. The most widely used scale is "Likert scale," which comprises response mainly in four categories of "strongly agree," "agree," "disagree" and "strongly disagree." The researcher will prepare number of variables or statements with categories of "strongly agree," "agree," "disagree," and "strongly disagree."

6. Analysis and Interpretation of Data

Analysis and interpretation of data are very crucial parts of research project. It requires skill and technical knowledge as to how to go about doing research. It can be done only by the researcher or by someone under the close supervision of the researcher. It requires knowledge about data, skill and the ability to bring into generalization. The researcher has to know the background, objects and hypothesis of the research. It is through systematic analysis and interpretation of data underlying features of research will be revealed and the researcher will be able to draw conclusion with valid generalization. Facts and figures cannot speak for themselves without analysis and interpretation. Only by organizing, analysing and interpreting data collected we can see the interrelationship, causes and connection of various parts of the research and will be able to move to the next steps of the research.

6.1. Steps in Analysis

There are mainly two steps of data analysis. First, data collected for research purpose has to be conceptualized corresponding to each aspect of phenomenon. Then they have to be tabulated for the aggregate group and provide general statistical or quantitative description. Second, similar data are tabulated in sub-groups, which are regarded significant. These sub-groups provide description of differentiated quantities as desired and at the same time population is redefined relevant to the problem.

7. Choice of Population

Choice of population may be defined a certain phenomenon consisting of sets of conceivable data or hypothetical data in the given intended research. It can be either finite population or infinite population. Whereas finite population consists of definite number of objects, infinite population consists of indefinitely large number of objects. Either finite or infinite, it is important for sampling to define the interest and needs of the people clearly and accurately under study. One example of finite population could be using phone to contact respondents which limit the representativeness of the persons that may not meet the requirement of selection criteria. This kind of selection of population will be possible if only the respondents have phone. So, the process of research will be limited to those who possess phone. However, such problem can be avoided by defining population as the total collection of elements actually available for sampling. In such scenario the words "group" or "aggregate" can be used to get close what the statisticians mean by population. But, it is always better for the researcher to be sure in getting available data before undertaking any research so that he/she need not face difficulty is pursuing the research, particularly in theological research.

8. Sampling Design

Mishra defines sampling design as "a sample design is a definite plan, completely defined before any data are collected, for obtaining a sample from a given population." There are certain steps to develop sample design as follows:

a. Sampling Unit: Before selecting sample, the sample unit must be decided. Sampling unit may be a geographical area like region, district, state, village etc. The researcher has to select one or more unit that one wants to study. It should not be too big that one cannot cover and may not be representative of the research undertaken.

b. Source List: Source list is very important for sampling design. This refers to the number of items to be collected from the universe. It contains names of all in the universe. The list of items of the universe must be comprehensive, correct and reliable. The researcher must keep in mind that it represents the population the best way as possible.

c. Size of Sample: The size of sample will depend on the length and breadth of the research. This refers to the number of items to be selected from the universe that will be representative and reliable with validity. The size of sample should be neither too small nor too large, so it should be optimum so that researcher can achieve the goal with efficiency with reliable representation, validity and flexibility.

9. Interpretation of Data

After analysing the data, the data have to be interpreted. Interpretation of data is an important part of the investigation. Interpretation involves drawing inferences from collected data or facts. It is an inevitable part of investigation, because only through interpretation we can derive meaning and draw inference that will lead to conclusion for solution of a particular problem under investigation. Without interpretation statistical facts or numbers do not have any validity and significance. When the facts or numbers are interpreted then only will it be possible to utilize them in the research undertaken. Proper interpretation of data will ensure usefulness of data and will provide certain conclusion to the problem under study.

9.1. Codification and Processing of Data

a. Codification

After analysing and interpreting the data collected, they have to be codified so that data can be easily identified. Coding is technical procedure by which data are categorized and transformed into symbols, generally in numerals and then tabulated and counted. Transforming into symbols does not happen automatically, it involves judgement on the part of the coder. Coding is done to reduce several replies into smaller number for effective analysis of the data, otherwise which may contain critical information that will become a difficult task for interpretation. It is better to do coding at the time of preparation of questionnaire, this will help in computer tabulation and make things easier. Coding can be done either through computer or by hand. In computer coding one can do straight forward, key punch from the questionnaire and in hand coding some standard methods have to be followed. One such standard method is to code in margin with coloured pencil and the other is to transcribe the data from questionnaire in a separate coding sheet. Whatever method is used one must ensure that coding errors are eliminated altogether or reduced to minimum level.

b. Data Processing

Data processing is another aspect that the researcher needs to take into account, while doing research. After collection of data, the researcher has to process the data and analyse in accordance with the outline of the research. Data processing has to align with the purpose of the research that was laid down in the beginning of the research. This is very essential part of the research for a scientific study, by which the researcher can ensure all the relevant information/data for comparison and analysis. Data processing involves editing, coding, classification of collected data in order to have amenable analysis. This process allows to create an "intelligible accounts" and enables to ask question like "What does it all mean?" for the given research.

Summary

In this chapter, we have discussed tabulation, analysis and interpretation of data. Without tabulation, analysis and interpretation, data remain mere numbers. Analysis and interpretation of data are very crucial parts of research project. In choice of population certain phenomenon consists of conceivable data or hypothetical data in the given intended research. For any research project sampling is very important, which is a defined plan, defined before any data are collected to obtain sample for given population. There are different types of tabulation, such as – pie chart, stacked bar chart, diagram, figure etc.

References

Evans, David, Paul Gruba and Justine Zobel. *How to Write Better Thesis.* 3rd edition, New York: Springer, 2014.

Kaufman, Roger, Ingrid Guerra and William A. Platt. *Practical Education for Educators: Finding What Works and What Doesn't.* California: Crown Press, 2006.

Kothari, C. S. *Research Methodology: Methods and Techniques,* 2nd edition. New Delhi: New Age International (P) Limited Publisher, 2004.

Kumar, Ranjit. *Research Methodology: A Step by Step Guide for Beginners.* 3rd edition. New Delhi, SAGE Publications India, Pvt Ltd, 2011.

Leavy, Patricia. *Research Design,* 2nd edition. New York: Guildford Press, a Division of Publications, Inc., 2023.

Mishra, R. P. *Research Methodology: A Hand Book.* New Delhi: Concept Publishing Company, 2001.

Nakkiran S, and G. Ramesh. *Research Method in Rural Development.* New Delhi: Deep & Deep Publications, PVT. LTD., 2009.

Sellitiz, Clair, Mark Jahoda, Morton Deutsch and Stuart W. Cook. *Research Methods in Social Relations,* Revised Edition. Delhi: Surjeet Publications, 2007.

Singh, Y. K. and R. B. Bajpai. *Research Methodology: Data Presentation.* New Delhi: APH Publishing Corporations, 2008.

Thakur, Devendra. *Research Methodology in Social Science.* New Delhi: Deep & Deep Publications PVT. LTD., 2003.

Edited Book

Schofield, "Survey Sampling" in *Data Collection and Analysis,* 2nd edition. Edited by Sapsford, Roger and Victor Jupp. London: SAGE Publications, 2006.

Chapter 13

Statistical Package for the Social Sciences (SPSS) and Analysis of Variance (ANOVA)

Introduction

This chapter deals with the use of a software generally called Statistical Package for the Social Sciences (SPSS), officially known as IBM SPSS Statistics Software and Analysis of Variance (ANOVA). ANOVA is already discussed in various ways in previous chapters. In this chapter, it will be dealt in descriptive and theoretical level. Both SPSS and ANOVA are very important methods of data analysis in any social research. The SPSS device is used widely in theological research for theological education. In fact, in the research of Christian ministry department SPSS has become integral part of research process. This chapter attempts to provide as to how to use SPSS at rudimentary and theoretical level. For the use of practical purposes, the researcher has to purchase SPSS software.

1. Statistical Package for the Social Sciences (SPSS)

SPSS is a software used for statistical analysis and data management both in quantitative and qualitative research, but primarily for quantitative research in social sciences. SPSS is widely used in social research to tabulate, analyse, interpret data. It is user-friendly and allows the researcher to enter, manage, transform data including handling of missing values and clearing data base. It aids in statistical procedure including descriptive statistics, inferential statistics (t-test, ANOVA and regression). It also provides tools for creating various types of charts and graphs to visualize data patterns and trends. User can easily generate reports with customized outputs, including tables, charts and statistical results. SPSS integrates with other software, including R and Python, for more advanced data analysis and programming. Computing power can be used for statistical reasoning, correct selection of stratified test, careful evaluation of underlying assumptions and cautious interpretation of results.

The 11th version of SPSS was one of the most comprehensive SPSS software. It can perform highly complex data manipulation and analysis with simple instruction. SPSS can read data almost in any format – numeric, alphanumeric, binary, dollar, date, time, format, and version 6 onwards can read files created using spreadsheet, such as, Excel or data base software. Besides these software guides and workbooks are available. Among them *SPSS Manuel, Analysis without Anguish,* and *Doing Statistics with SPSS* are notable (For step by step guide for analysis, see Punch, 2005, Appendix 1). The latest version of IBM SPSS statistics 30.0.0 software was released on September 30, 2024.

1.1. How to Handle Variables and their Values in SPSS

The first step in SPSS is to label the variables and place or input the obtained data into their respective variable column. The researcher has to name variables before inputting data. In SPSS the researcher not only label each variable but gives abbreviated name. For example, 'qualif' for qualification and 'ethnog' for an ethnic group. Then it also labels each group into full name to make print out clear. For example, if the researcher is going to create a column for data relating to qualification of theological teachers and asked to indicate their highest theological qualification by giving five qualification to choose 1 through 5, then example procedure would be as follows:

a. Select the column the researcher wishes to label with variable. To select the column the researcher needs to make sure that he/she cursor and activated cell is framed in bold in that column.
b. Then the researcher needs to click in Data from the menu bar to produce a drop-down menu.
c. On the drop-down menu, he/she needs to select *Define Variable*, which opens *Define Variable* dialogue box.
d. *Variable Label:* Variable label can have up to eight characters in length, so *var00001* (SPSS default label), which represented the qualification of the teachers will be abbreviated '*qualif*' by typing in '*qualif*' which will delete the highlighted default name '*var00001* in the variable name: box.
e. Next click on the *Label* button to display the *Define Label* box.
f. In the *Variable Label* box, type the full variable name 'qualification.'
g. Then in the *Values* space type figure '1' and in the *Value Label* type '*Certificate.*'
h. Then select *Add* which puts 1,00 = 'certificate' in the bottom box. Repeat this procedure for the four values

of 2 for 'diploma,' 3 for 'bachelor of divinity,' 4 for 'master of theology,' and 5 for 'doctor of theology.'

i. When all the coding is complete, select *Continue*, then *OK*. The first column is now labelled *'qualif'* and is ready for data entry. Now the output will show the full name and related coding.

1.2. Use of SPSS for Descriptive Statistics

Percentage and Frequencies

To access percentage and frequencies through the use of SPSS, the following steps can be followed:

a. Click the *statistic* on the menu bar.
b. From the drop-down menu select *Summarize*, then click on *Frequencies*. This opens the *Frequencies* dialogue box.
c. Highlight the variables for which the researcher wishes to generate descriptive statistics and use the arrow button to place them in '*Variables*': box.
d. Select *'Statistics,'* which brings the *'Frequencies Statistics'* box into display.
e. In the *Dispersion area* click *Minimum* and *Maximum.*
f. Choose *Continue,* then *OK* to obtain output.

1.3. Use of SPSS in Graph

Data can be presented in graph through in the form of bar chart, pie chart or histogram that helps in understanding and bring out salient features of a mass of figure in visual summary. For example, to create a pie, the following steps can be followed:

a. Click *Graph* then select *Pie.*
b. Click *Summaries for Groups of Cases.*

c. Select *Define* in the *Define Pie. Summarize for Group Cases* box, highlight the variable of interest and move it to the *Define Slices* box.
d. Click *OK* and the chart will be displayed.
e. To add percentage to the slice, double click on the chart to select for editing.
f. Select *Charts* then *Option.*
g. In the *Pie* chart *Options* box click next to present in the *Label* box.
h. Select *Format* then click on the down arrow next to *Position* and select *Numbers Inside, Text Outside.*
i. Choose *Continue* then *OK* to display the edited pie chart.

1.4. Descriptive Statistics

In the use of SPSS in descriptive statistics the following steps can be followed.

a. Click on *Statistics* to display a drop-down menu.
b. From this menu, select *Summarize* then *Explore* to obtain *Explore* dialogue box.
c. Transfer to the Dependent list box, by clicking and highlighting those variables for which you wish to obtain the descriptive statistics.
d. In the *Display* box choose Statistics.
e. Click on the *Statistics* button, which will bring the *Explore: Statistics* dialogue box into view.
f. Make sure *Descriptive* is chosen. Select *Continue* and then *OK* to produce output.

1.5. Creating Box Plot

A box plot can present a clear visual expression of a set of data and can be used instead of histogram and bar charts. The following steps can be followed:

a. Click *Graph,* then *Boxplot* to produce the *Boxplot* dialogue box.
b. Select *Simple* then click on *Summarize of Groups of Cases.*
c. Select *Define* to display the *Define Simple Boxplot; Summarize* box.
d. Choose your quantitative variable(s) by highlighting and clicking the arrow button to transfer to the variable box.
e. Choose your qualitative variable, move it to the *Category Axis* box.
f. Finally select *OK* and then box plot is displayed.

2. Analysis of Variance (ANOVA)

ANOVA is a hypothesis for testing procedure used to determine differences that exist in two or more samples or treatment of research. The purpose is to decide whether differences between samples or treatment is simply due to chance (sampling error) or there are systematic effects that have caused scores in one group to be different scores from the scores in other groups. It is a statistical method used to compare means of two or more variance within and between groups. It determines whether there is observed differences between means of groups are statistically significant or likely due to random chance. ANOVA is essentially a generalization of t-test for comparison of multiple groups.

Burns offers an example, where a psychologist conducts an experiment on three students on the effect of sound/ noise in reading, say noise condition is – silent, background music and loud music. Null hypothesis would propose that there are no significant differences in the effect of sound/ noise between three groups in learning. However, the alternative hypothesis would state different noise conditions significantly effect in learning. With intuition or common sense, one may come to conclusion that those who studied in silence perform significantly better than the other two groups. This hypothesis may be proved wrong because even those who studied with loud music did equally good with those who studied in silence. So, the social scientist will not accept the hypothesis based on intuition or common sense until proper analysis is done, because there could be different possibilities of hypotheses.

3. T-test

A t-test is statistical test used to compare the means (average) of two groups or sample of data. A t-test is inferential statistic to determine whether there is statistically significant difference between two means of variables. T-test is suitable for situation where primary focus is on direct comparison between two groups. There are three types of t-test – the one sample t-test, the two samples t-test and paired t-test.

4. Variance

In both statistic and accounting, variance measures the spread of deviation of data points from average or expected values. Variance in simple term means is measurement of a set of numbers, how much it spread out or dispersed from their average (mean). Simply put variance means 'difference' or 'variation.' For example, mean (2,4,9,2), 2+4+9+2/4 = 4.25, variance for (2,4,9,2) is 2+4+9+2/4 = 4.25 or (2– 4.25) square + (4– 4.25) square + (9 – 4.25) square + (2 – 4.25) square/4 = 6.68

5. Mean

Mean means the average value of a set of numbers. It is a quantitative representation of variables, representing the centre of a collection of numbers and intermediate to the extreme set values of a set of numbers. In statistic it also known as average. In simple term 'mean' is used for 'middle' of a set of data. For example, mean for numbers 6,7,4, 3, 5 = 5, 6+7+4+3+5 = 25, 25/5=5. Here the 5 is mean or middle or we can say average.

Summary

SPSS is a software used for statistical analysis and data management in both quantitative and qualitative research. It is widely used in social science research to tabulate, analyse and interpret data. ANOVA is a hypothesis for testing procedure used to determine differences that exist in two or more samples. The purpose is to decide the difference between samples and treatment. T-test is statistical test used to compare the means (average) of two groups or sample of data. Variance means measurement of a set of numbers that are spread out and dispersed from the average or expected values. Mean means the average value of a set of numbers. It is quantitative representation of numbers. It is also called "average" or "middle" in statistical analysis.

References

Burns, B. Robert. *Introduction to Research Methods,* Fourth Edition. London; Thousand Oaks; New Delhi: SAGE Publications, 2000.

Punch, Keith F. *Introducing to Social Research: Quantitative and Qualitative Approaches,* Third Edition. Los Angeles; London; New Delhi: SAGE Publications, 2005.

Chapter 14

Ethics of Inquiry in Social Research

Introduction

All social research involves ethical issues, because it involves data collection from people, and about people. Ethics of inquiry specifically focuses on the analysis of ethical issues that are raised when people are involved as participants. Without ethical implication, there is every possibility of manipulating data in favour of the researcher. Therefore, a researcher must adhere to the guidelines or principles for ethical conduct in the research process. Ethics are self-regulatory guidelines for making decision and defining profession by establishing ethical codes, professional organization for maintaining the integrity of the profession, expected conduct of members and protection of welfare of the subjects and clients. Ethical codes give researcher direction when confronting ethical dilemmas or confusing situation.

1. Principles of Ethics of Inquiry

1.1. Ethical Codes of Research

For the conduct of research, various professionals, association, government agencies and universities have created specific codes, rules and policies relating research ethics. A researcher needs to abide by these specific codes, rules and policies enacted by various professionals, government agencies, theological institutions and universities.

1.2. Voluntary Participation

There are researches where subjects will participate voluntarily. The principle of voluntary participation requires that participants do not feel forced or threatened while participating. This is especially relevant where researcher had previously replied on 'captive audience' for their subjects, such as prisons, universities, schools, colleges etc. For empirical study in theological education, participation either in interview, focus group or questionnaire, particularly in Christian ministry is always voluntary.

1.3. Informed Consent

Informed consent means that we may carry out our research, ask our questions, organize focus groups, participate in community projects and so on, only after explaining the community, why we are doing this research and what are the intended outcome for both ourselves and for them. After obtaining consent from the people we should proceed with our research project. The researcher must obtain explicit or implicit informed consent of their subjects to take part in an investigation. An explanation should be given to the subjects about the general purpose of the research and who is sponsoring. They should be told that their participation in the research is voluntary and they can withdraw at any time if they wish. They also should be informed the possible risk that can harm them. In any case written consent form can be issued and get an agreement signed by the subject or guardian.

1.4. Debriefing

Debriefing means informing the subjects about the nature of the study without any deception. It should be done by arranging a session with the subjects. The researcher must be able to restore subjects' self-esteem and trust in the process of study.

1.5. Privacy and Confidentiality

Maintaining privacy and confidentiality of informants or subjects is a must on the part of the researcher. There are two standards that can be applied in order to help participants to protect their privacy and confidentiality. First, the researchers can guarantee the participants confidentiality and assure that their identity will not be made public. Second, in a stricter standard is the principle of anonymity, which means that participants will remain anonymous throughout the study, even to the researchers themselves. The anonymity guarantee is a stronger privacy. But sometime it is difficult to accomplish, especially in a situation, where participants have to be measured at multiple times.

1.6. Right to Discontinue

The researcher must give room for the participants the right to discontinue if they wish. The researcher has to respect the decision of the participants. It is an important safeguard. It is normally applied in questionnaire or interview when the respondents refuse to respond certain questions. Therefore, the researcher must be able to conduct the research in a careful and tactful way.

1.7. Experimental Obligation

Researchers make several implicit obligations to the participants, for example, participants agree to be present at a specific time and place, then the researcher must be also there at the place on time. If the researcher has promised to send a summary report of the results of the subjects then it must be done. The researcher must not run overtime as the subjects may have other prior engagement and commitment right after the interview or any activity related to research.

2. Social Responsibility of the Researcher

There is social responsibility of the researcher that transcends the academic discipline or profession that needs to be attended. The ultimate goal of any research is to contribute to greater public interest and common good. It is important to carry out research in a way that enhances public perception and attitude toward research. The ethical responsibility of the researcher is not to spoil the others but invest time and energy with care and attention to end the research project from the start.

2.1. Avoidance of Harm to Respondents

The researcher has social responsibility to protect the participants, for physical, social and psychological well-being. One needs to assess the possible risk or costs of respondents taking part in the research. The researcher must try to minimize the cost but at the same time weigh against the benefits to individual and wider group. It is difficult to judge the impact of any research one undertakes and any benefit for the respondents. If the researcher feels that people may be harmed then he/she should not continue with the research. The first right of any participant in the research project is the right to safety. Any research that endangers human life or physical health is unacceptable in any research. It is more so in theological research. Now a days even harming animal in the process of research, although it may benefit human, is discouraged. (Miller, 1985, Rollin, 1985 and Tannenbaum and Rowan, 1985).

2.2. Wasting Peoples' Time

Any research undertaken requires time and energy, but the researcher must see that he/she does not waste people's time, which will hamper in household income. If substantial time is taken away from the participants, it is always good to give compensation. The researcher must be concerned with the completion of the research on the hand and people's time on the other.

2.3. Raising Expectation

In any research there are expectations both from the researchers and the participants. At times it may be too high that you cannot fulfil but other time too low that you yourself need extra motivation. The researcher should not provide too high expectation but on the other hand must see that the research is beneficial to the participants. It is not that easy to strike a balance. It is particularly difficult which is connected with socio-economic development.

2.4. Avoidance of Undue Intrusion

The researcher must make sure that the research work does not lead to undue intrusion. On the part of the researcher, it is easy to get excited about how important the research work is, but it is also essential to remember that respondents have their priorities in their life. The researcher needs to consider how potentially the research can be intrusive to the respondents. Particularly, there should not be any element that will lead to intrusion in private and family matters. The pursuit to get information does not justify overriding other social and cultural values.

2.5. Avoidance of Deception

In social science research there has been a debate, whether or not a researcher under what circumstances, can deceive. Deception is the most controversial aspect in the social research. Social scientists say in certain cases deception is unavoidable, especially dealing with health issues. In such cases true purpose of investigation may not be revealed. For example, in the study of relationship between smoking and lung cancer, if the investigator reveals the true purpose, the researcher may not get the desired outcome. Again, sociologists opine that the study on behaviour, such as – aggression, conformity, cheating etc. will not be possible without some form of deception. However, psychologist Diana Baumrind (1985) strongly opposes any deception arguing that intentional deception is unethical, because it violets the implicit trust in between investigator-subject-relationship. This particular ethical implication of deception arose from psychological experimentation. Among the psychologists, the consensus is that, sometime some form of deception is unavoidable in experiment and consequently there are literatures how to apply it in experimental research. In case in some researches, if some form of deception is unavoidable, psychologists have suggested the followings:

a. Debrief as soon as possible after the research.
b. Carry out the debriefing slowly and carefully, making sure that subjects understood what was going on.
c. Express their discomfort about using such techniques.
d. Point out that in a good experiment everyone is fooled.

2.6. Respondents' Right to Data and Publication

In social science research, it is important to recognize the rights of respondents over data and publication a researcher produces. It is good practice, where possible, to allow respondents to see the transcripts of interview and field-notes and alter the content, withdraw statement and provide additional information, if they so wish. It can be carried out verbally also. However, upsetting it is to the researcher to lose good data, if a respondent does not want the researcher to publish, one should not use it. The question of feedback and consultation on action or publication arising from the researcher is also an ethical one. Respondents are entitled to know what the researcher is saying about them.

2.7. Informing Respondents

The respondents should be informed well ahead of time about the purpose of the research, because it involves voluntary cooperation and participation. It is a basic premise of ethical survey. Respondents should have the following rights, before being asked to answer questions:

a. The name of the organization that carrying out the research. If an interview is involved, the respondent also should have the interviewer.
b. The sponsorship that is, who is supporting or paying for the research.
c. Assurance that cooperation or participation is voluntary and there will be no negative consequences to those decide not to participate.
d. Assurance that respondents can skip any question that they do not want to answer.

2.8. Protecting Respondents

The main issue with respect to protecting respondents is the way in which the information they provide will be treated. The followings are some standard procedures that the researcher can follow carefully to minimize the breach of trust and confidentiality:

a. All people who have access to the data or a role in data collection should be committed in writing to confidentiality.
b. Complete interview schedule should not be accessible to non-project members.
c. Identifiers should be removed from completed questionnaire if non-staff people are going to look at them; it is common to remove them as soon as possible in any case.
d. During analysis, researchers should be careful about presenting data for very small categories of people who might be identifiable.

Summary

In any research project, the researcher must strictly adhere to the principles of inquiry. Various professionals, associations, government, agencies, and universities have their own ethical codes of research, which the researcher must know before doing research on those institutions. In any research, participation must be voluntary. No participant should be forced, compelled or coerced to participate. Before conducting research, consent from the participants must be obtained. Participants must be briefed by explaining the purpose of research before undertaking any research. Maintaining privacy and confidentiality of participants is utmost important on the part of the researcher. At any moment the participants have the right to discontinue in the research process without any contempt. There are social responsibilities that a researcher needs to look into, such as avoidance of harm, wasting people's time, avoiding undue intrusion and respondent's right to data and publication.

References

Cohen, Louis, Lawrence Manion and Keith Morrison. *Research Method in Education,* 5th edition. London: Taylor & Francis Group, 2005.

Joseph, A. Anthony. *Methodology for Research: Guide for Writing Dissertation, Theses, and Scientific Papers.* Bangalore: Theological Publications in India, 1986.

Kothari, C. R. *Research Methodology: Methods and Technique,* 2nd edition. New Delhi: New International (p), Publishers, 2004.

Mabry, Hunter. *A Manual for Researchers and Writers,* Revised Edition. Bangalore: BTESSC, 2018.

Miller, Robert L. and John D. Brewer. *The A-Z of Social Research.* London: SAGE Publications, 2003,

Nakkiran, S. and G. Ramesh. *Research Method in Rural Development.* New Delhi: Deep and Deep Publications PVT. LTD, 2009.

Sellitiz, Claire, Marie Jahoda, Morton Deutsch and Stuart W. Cook. *Research Method in Social Relations,* Revised Edition. Delhi: Surjeet Publications, 2007.

Swain, A. K. P. C. *Research Methodology: Theory and Practice.* New Delhi: Kalyani Publishers, 2016.

Singleton, A. Royce and Bruce C. Straits. *Approaches to Social Research.* New York; Oxford: Oxford University Press, 1999.

Chapter 15

Qualitative Research in Theological Education

Introduction

This chapter deals primarily with the qualitative method in social and theological research. Although, we have dealt briefly about qualitative method in chapter three, in this chapter, the method is discussed more elaborately with certain methodologies that are already in place but which need to be revisited in theological education. Ever since the emergence of social science research method, quantitative method has gained primacy over qualitative research, to the extent that students are reluctant to undertake qualitative inquiry within the fraternity of Senate of Serampore College (University) with an inhibition that their research may not be accepted, particularly in Christian Ministry (mainly Christian education and Counselling). Statistical analysis and numbering have become near absolute in Christian ministry research. As a result, dissertation becomes voluminous with quantitative analysis and cover more space than other materials. Qualitative analysis is mainly confined within literature review and theoretical/conceptual framework developed by various theorists. These aspects are inalienable parts in research but more emphasis is given to questionnaire, its analysis, tabulation, chart, diagram etc. Quantitative method is a tool to support and enhance qualitative aspect of the research in theological education, not vice versa. To enrich qualitative aspect of empirical study the following methods are taken into consideration for discussion.

1. Ecological Psychology Method

In the wake of environmental crisis, ecological psychology method has become popular in social science research. This is qualitative research. Robert Barker and Herbert Wright (1967) are the ones who developed ecological psychology method in social science. This method heavily relies on natural history and field studies. In this method human and environment are seen interconnected and interdependent. This method begins with pure and detailed description of individual, community and environment. Here the role of the researcher is not one of participant but of 'spectator,' where the researcher observes phenomenon and the 'streams of behaviour' are analysed in terms of assumed goal-oriented actions.

The ecological metaphor or paradigm also can offer ecological clinical research that seeks to understand the patient's concern within the context of his/her life world that is the personal life of the patient, family, community and ecological concern. In this research the unit of analysis is primarily individual (in case of patient) but it can be applied in delivering qualities of community life. This approach provides potential in the evaluation of the programmes of organization or community related to environmental/ ecological crisis.

In this research, the researcher focuses on central features of behavioural setting. He/she observes the particular constellation of place, things and time that constitute a definitive environment. Ecological psychologists begin their research on a detailed and qualitative description based on observation in natural environment. Then they codify and analyse the finding in quantitative procedure. Segments of goal-directed behaviour settings and characteristics are coded numerically and analysed statistically. In this method the researcher goes from thick description of qualitative data to quantitative analysis, not vice versa. One cannot generate thick description and qualitative narrative from original quantitative data. Therefore, the researcher has to move from qualitative to quantitative. In this approach, in some cases research can be done without quantification.

The focus of ecological psychology method is on the relationship between human behaviour and environment. This method also provides good transition to the next perspective of other disciplines. Thus, it facilitates system theory which is more comprehensive and interdisciplinary in examining the context of human action in different developmental programmes of organization and communities.

In the context of indigenous community (Tribals, Adivasis etc.) this method is readily applicable to understand the interconnected and interdependent relationship between human being and environment. The concern of ecology has become one of the major issues in theological education.

2. Constructionism and Constructivism

Constructivism begins with the premise that human world is different from natural world. Guba and Lincoln, (1990) argue that physical world must be studied differently. The fundamental assumption to this argument is that human being has the ability to interpret and construct reality. That interpretation and construction take place in a day to day life through interaction and engagement embedded in socio-cultural life. Social scientists believe that human perception is not real as the natural world is real. Human perception of things and reality differ from individual to individual and from culture to culture. Just like sun and moon are absolute and real, human perception cannot be absolute and final. Human perception is 'made up' and shaped by cultural and linguistic construct. That construction of reality will be in variance, so no one can claim my perception is the absolute and final. Therefore, in qualitative research, the researcher owns his/her conclusion and acknowledges the fact it is under the subject of scrutiny. However, when a researcher says that human perception is not real as sun and moon, it does not mean that it is not perceived and experienced as real by real people. In this regard W.I. Thomas' theorem that says "*What is defined or perceived by people as real is real in its consequences*" is relevant (Thomas and Thomas, 1928). Constructivist studies multiple realities constructed by people and derive implication from those construction for the people. Those construction takes place through interaction and relationship in the community and society.

Shadish (1995), thus sums up constructivism by saying, it "refers to constructing *knowledge about* reality, not constructing reality itself." In other words, constructivism does not construct reality but construct knowledge about reality. Constructivists assume that human beings do not have singular access to reality. Humans do not have stable and full knowledge about external reality. All our understandings are contextually embedded and constructed and the reality is interpersonally forged and it is necessarily limited in time and space. According to constructivism truth is formed by consensus among the sophisticated constructor. It does not necessarily correspond with the objective reality. The understanding of objective has no meaning except within the framework of some values. It believes that objective cannot be assessed fully from any position.

3. Narratology or Narrative Analysis

Todoror was the one who coined the term *narratology* in 1969. The objective was to elevate form of object knowledge for a new science. Narratology or narrative analysis is one of the qualitative inquiries. Narratology or narrative analysis is becoming more popular again in academics recently. It has become an inalienable part of academics among the subaltern groups, such as – Tribals, Dalits, Adivasis and Women. They want to narrate their histories, stories, experiences in order to build agency and to form subject constitution. Narratology method includes in-depth interview, transcripts, life story, historical memoir and creative non-fiction stories. Narrative studies are influenced by phenomenology in its understanding of lived experiences and perception of their day to day life experiences.

It deals with personal, community narrative, graffiti, literary non-fiction and histories. These materials reveal cultural and social patterns through the lens of individual and community experience. The narrative inquiry is qualitative inquiry. This method helps in studying and analysing the connection between psychological, cultural, sociological and political conditions and human experience of a community. Robert Coles (1989), Harvard professor of psychiatry opines that narratology can be basis for teaching, learning and moral reflection. Michael White and David Easton (1990) suggest how narratives/stories can be means of therapy. They opine that people have adjustment difficulties because the story of their life that has created by either themselves or others does not match with their lived experiences. There is disconcertedness between their perception and reality of lived experiences. The purpose of therapist is to help people to reorient narrative by guiding them to re-write their stories. Contemporary anthropologists and feminists often emphasize the study of lives from the narrator's point of view, with data seen as shared production with researcher (Manning and Cullum-Swan, 1994). It is also used in medical and illness studies (Brody, 1987; Coles, 1989), in studies of major life events and traumatic experience (Riessman, 1993), in studies in education both from students' and teachers' point of view.

4. Phenomenology

Phenomenology as a philosophical discipline was first used by German philosopher Edmund H. Husserl (1859-1938). Then Alfred Schutz applied this methodology in social perspective in 1977. Therefore, Schutz was the one who first applied the methodology of phenomenology in social research. Then on different disciplines started to use phenomenological method across the fields of different disciplines, including theological education.

By phenomenology what Husserl meant was that people describe things and experiences through their senses made out of phenomena that they encounter in their day to day life. His most philosophical thought was, *We can only know what we experience by attending to perception and meaning.* It was in one way philosophically pragmatist. Van Menon (1990) defines phenomenology that makes some "'thing,' what it is and without which it could not be what it is." It asks the very nature of a phenomenon.

The term 'phenomenology' has become so popular across the fields of different disciplines to the extent that sometime its meaning is lost and people are confused what really it means. Creswell (1989) claims that phenomenology is primarily used in qualitative research. Phenomenological method is used in sociology and psychology .for the study of groups or individuals.

The main focus of phenomenology or phenomenography is to explore how human beings make sense of their experiences and transform both individual and community. It is done through shared meaning in the process of interaction and encounter. It involves how people comprehend thoroughly and describe, perceive, judge, remember and make sense out of a particular phenomenon. All these create collective consciousness that guides and preserves community mores and ethos. It does reflection but that reflection is not *introspective* but rather *retrospective.* It reflects on the passed and lived experiences.

There are primarily two implications in the study of phenomenology. The first implication is that "what is important to know is what people experience and how they interpret the world." The second implication is methodological one, that says "The only way for us really know what another person experience is to experience the phenomenon as directly as ourselves." This leads to participant observation that we have discussed earlier.

5. Heuristic Inquiry

Heuristic inquiry is relatively recent approach/method to social science. It is qualitative research in nature. The term heuristic is derived from Greek word *heureisken,* which means 'to discover or to find.' It was Moustakas, who developed heuristic inquiry. It is a form of phenomenological inquiry that foregrounds personal experience and insights in any research undertaking. Although, it is one form of phenomenological inquiry it differs from it in four major ways. The first difference is, heuristic inquiry emphasizes in the interconnection and relationship in the research undertaken, while phenomenological inquiry detaches itself in analysing an experience. Second, heuristic inquiry depicts essential meanings and portray in intrigue and personal significance that imbue researcher to know. In other words, this inquiry depicts essential meaning and attach great significance to researcher's knowledge. The third difference is that it concludes that intuition and tacit understanding of the researcher is very important for the development of 'creative synthesis.' But phenomenological inquiry distils the structure of experience. It does not take the experience of the researcher in toto but scrutinizes. The fourth difference is in the process of descriptive analysis, phenomenology loses the person (the subject) but in heuristic research, the research participants remain visible in the process of research. The researchers (the subjects) do not lose their identity. Phenomenology ends with essence of experience but heuristic inquiry retains the essence of the persons in experience.

There are two focuses in heuristic inquiry, first the researcher must have intense interest in the phenomenon under study. Second, if there is any correspondence then it must share the intensity of experience. It focuses on intense human experience. It is combination of the understanding of essence of the phenomenon. Heuristic inquiry is concerned with meaning, not measurement, in the essence, not in appearance, in quality, not in quantity, with experience, not with behaviour (Douglass and Moustakas, 1985).

In heuristic study reports are piled up with discoveries and reflection of the researcher. The essence of heuristic inquiry is to foreground the personal experience, insights, and reflection of the researcher on the phenomenon undertaken for study. The researcher understands the essence of phenomenon through reflection and inquiry with the co-researchers (if there is any). There is interconnection between the researcher and co-researchers.

The vitality of heuristic inquiry comes from systematic observation of the researcher through dialogue between oneself and others. This creates an understanding that an individual can live deeply and passionately with the moment one encounters. In heuristic inquiry the researcher is fully immersed in the phenomenon and engages with the mysteries and miracles of the phenomenon. The systematic steps taken by the researcher lead to definitive exploration of experiential essence. The important aspect of heuristic inquiry is that it epitomizes the phenomenological meanings and knowing through personal experiences. It is primarily qualitative inquiry.

6. Emic Approach in Social Research

Emic inquiry is another approach that is becoming popular again in social research. Due to increasing assertion of the subaltern groups, such as - Tribals, Dalits, Adivasis and Women who want to narrate their own histories, stories and experiences, the emic approach is surfacing again across the fields of theology, Christian education, hermeneutics, women studies etc. Emic approach is an approach from insiders' perspective. On the other hand, etic is an approach from the outsiders' perspective. During modern and colonial period missionaries, colonial administrators, anthropologists or historians were pioneer in the study of so-called native people. They were the "objects" of inquiry and written about without any agency.

Kenneth L. Pike was the first to coin the concept of emic-etic in the Summer Institute of Linguistic (SIL) in 1982 from the perspective of phonetic and phonemics. He then actively adopted the concept in various fields beside anthropology, such as – cross-cultural psychology and organizational studies.

Emic approach studies any culture or problem from the perspective of insiders and etic approach studies from the perspective of outsiders. Franz Boas and Edward Sapir claimed that, a meaningful investigation of any culture can be done only by those who are from the same culture. However, it must be admitted that studying one particular culture only from insider's perspective will not suffice. Therefore, there is a need of cross-cultural analysis that can make distinction across cultures. An insider's view is not only to view what is happening, not only sees, but also feels. Obtaining something of the understanding of an insider, is however, can be considered, for most researchers, only a first step.

There is tension between these two approaches. The task of the researcher is to strike a balance between these two approaches through dialogue, negotiation and critic. The task of the researcher is to strike a balance between perceived universalistic (etic) and relativistic (emic) approaches. There has to be collaborative effort both by solo and collaborative participants in order to obtain authentic and reliable result.

7. Ethnomethodology

Harold Garfinkel (1967) was the one who developed ethnomethodology, while working with Yale cross-cultural studies. In his studies he came across with such labels as "ethnobotany," "ethnophysiology," and "ethnophysics." Then he developed "ethnomethodology" wherein *ethno* refers to the "availability to a number common-sense knowledge of his [her] society as a common-sense of the "whatever" (Turner 1994). Wallace and Wolf defined ethnomethodology as follows: "If we translated "ethno" part of the term as members (of a group)) or 'folk' or 'people,' then the term's meaning can be stated 'members' method of making sense of their social world." Ethnomethodology sets out to study 'folk' (ethno) and methods (methodology) for organizing the world as people comprehend (Silverman).

Ethnomethodology studies the social order by combining a phenomenological sensibility to every social practice (Gubrium and Holstein, 2000). Ethnomethodology studies deeply the norms, understanding and assumption of people group or a community that are taken for granted. Ethnomethodologists try to understand the phenomena people do not think about. They study why people do what they do. This methodology is rooted in phenomenology. The purpose of this study is not why but how people do what they do. It is about how people get things done, how they transform situation and how they preserve. It also sheds light how a stranger can learn to become routinely functioning member of a group, programmes and culture. For this Ethnomethodologists conduct in depth interview as participant observants. They do it in nonmanipulative and unobtrusive strategies. Ethnomethodologists have special interest in observing things naturally occurring by which people make sense out of what is happening in and through community life. In certain cases, Ethnomethodologists attempt to make knowledge explicit, what is called "tacit-knowledge."

Heuristic inquiry focuses on issues of intense personal interest, but ethnomethodology focuses on the ordinary and routine day to day life. In sum, Ethnomethodologists "bracketed or suspend their own belief in reality to study the reality of everyday life" (Taylor and Bogdan, 1984).

8. Grounded Theory

Grounded theory is not a theory *per se* but a method, an approach and strategy of social research. The purpose of grounded theory is to generate theory from data. The grounded theory is grounded on data. The objective of collecting and analyzing data is to generate theory. It is overall a strategy for doing research. It follows set of techniques and procedures. The style of data analysis is used to produce and develop a theory grounded in data.

The history of grounded theory can be traced back to five key publications. First, in 1960s Glaser and Strauss collectively published two landmark books in 1967 in medical sociology titled *The Discovery of Grounded Theory* after publishing *Awareness of Dying.* It has three purposes, to offer rational for grounded theory, to suggest logic for and specific grounded theories and to legitimize careful qualitative research.

In the same year after publication Glaser and Strauss taught grounded theory style of inquiry in seminar in qualitative analysis at the University of California in San Francisco. After 11 years, the second book *Theoretical Sensitivity* was published by Glaser in 1978. After nine years the third work *Qualitative Analysis for Social Scientists* was published by Strauss in 1987. The fourth publication was *Basics of Qualitative Research* by Strauss and Corbin with the subtitled *Grounded Theory Procedures and Technique* in 1990. Then Glaser published a book that critiqued Strauss' work titled *Basics of Grounded Theory Analysis* with the subtitle *Emergence vs Forcing* in 1992, which is the fifth publication. These five publications are the basic foundation of grounded theory.

There are some specific features in grounded theory: its explicit purpose is to generate theory through collected data but this basic feature raises contrast between research which aims to generate theory and research which aims to verify theory – so contrast between generation vs verification. In traditional quantitative research the general procedure as discussed in chapter two is theory verification based on hypothesis. But grounded theory approach which aims to generate theory, no 'up-front' theory is proposed and no hypothesis formulated. In other words, grounded theory as a qualitative research does not require prior theory and hypothesis. Because this approach does not start with theory from which hypothesis is deduced. It starts with open mind, aiming to end in a theory. So, it is theory of generative vs verification. This is where a lot of arguments come in theological education, even in Christian ministry. If the research in Christian ministry is qualitative in nature based on grounded theory than hypothesis and quantification are not required.

The second distinctive feature is in relation between data collection and data analysis which leads to theoretical sampling. In traditional quantitative research data collection is a discrete stage. Data collection is paramount in traditional/quantitative research. But in grounded theory data collection pattern is different. In grounded theory different sets of data collection may be required, first probably small, the second set of data will be after the analysis of first set of data. This is a theoretical principle. Depending on the nature of research more than two sets of data collection may be required. Paradoxically, if a satisfactory theory already exists, then, there is no need to collect data.

The place of grounded theory in social research can be seen mainly in five reasons: it is concerned with more on *how* to generate theory, second, it is coordinated, sympathetic but a the same time flexible in overall strategy, third, it brings a disciplined and organized system in the analysis of qualitative data, fourth, there are impressive demonstration of what grounded theory can produce in research and fifth, the generation approach grounded theory has much to recommend in the new areas of research. Because, new areas of research lack grounded concepts for discussing and explaining new research area (for a detailed discussion on the procedure of grounded theory data analysis, see chapter 10, Punch: 2005).

Summary

In the wake of environmental crisis, ecological psychology method has become popular across the fields of different disciplines to address the environmental concern. This method relies heavily on natural history and field studies. In this method human and environment are seen interconnected and interdependent. Constructionism or Constructivism studies views human world in a different way from natural world. Constructivists believe human perception is not real as natural world. It depends on person to person and culture to culture. This method constructs knowledge about reality but does not construct reality itself. Narratology or narrative analysis is another qualitative research, where people narrate their histories, stories, and experiences in order to build agency and subject constitution. We see its use widely among the subaltern groups, such as - Tribals, Dalits, Adivasis and Women, where they want to narrate their histories, stories and experiences. Phenomenology is qualitative inquiry that sees the world as it is, how people perceive themselves, how people make sense out of their experiences through the process of interaction and engagement. It involves how people comprehend a particular phenomenon and how they describe, judge, remember and make sense out of a particular phenomenon. Heuristic methodology is a form of phenomenological inquiry that foregrounds personal experiences and insights in research. It gives noticeable consideration in the intense personal experience in the process of inquiry. Emic inquiry is a method, where research is done from the perspective of an insider. An insider's view is not only to view what is happening, not only to see but also to feel. Ethnomethodology is rooted in phenomenology. It